STEPHEN HAWKING
A COMPLETE BIOGRAPHY

AF552872

MAHESH DUTT SHARMA

Published by
PRABHAT PRAKASHAN PVT. LTD.
4/19 Asaf Ali Road,
New Delhi-110 002 (INDIA)
e-mail: prabhatbooks@gmail.com

ISBN 978-93-5521-882-7
STEPHEN HAWKING: A COMPLETE BIOGRAPHY
by Mahesh Dutt Sharma

Edition
First, 2025

Price
₹ 350 (Rupees Three Hundred and Fifty only)

Printed at
Japan Art, Delhi

To all those
Whose extraordinary desire,
Formidable courage and uncommon willpower
Overcame all physical disabilities
And were able to achieve something in life.

Author's Note

While physics and mathematics may tell us how the universe began, they are not much use in predicting human behavior because there are far too many equations to solve. I'm no better than anyone else at understanding what makes people tick, particularly women.

There are too many accidents that can befall life on a single planet.

No one undertakes research in physics with the intention of winning a prize. It is the joy of discovering something no one knew before.

My goal is simple. It is a complete understanding of the universe, why it is as it is and why it exists at all.

—Stephen Hawking

The renowned Physicist, Stephen William Hawking, was born in Oxford, England to Frank and Isobel Hawking (as their eldest son with three other children) on January 8, 1942, presumably on the 300th anniversary of the death of Galileo. Hawking, a thinker amongst thinkers (his mother being an Oxford graduate, and father being a respected medical researcher), since his adolescence exhibited a penchant for science and the universe. His family has been described as an eccentric one, where everyone would have a book at the dinner table; they owned a taxi for a family car; they would breed bees; and so on and so forth. Frank Hawking wanted his son to show interest in the field of medicine, but Stephen had an ardent longing for cosmology as he was irresistibly drawn towards stars. Contrary to the popular opinion, academically Hawking was not an exceptional student, but only a bright and average one. As a teenager, Hawking, along with his friends, constructed a computer, commendably so, out of the recycled parts for cracking basic mathematical equations. In his own words, Hawking didn't put much time into his studies, as he was also interested in dance, sports, games, etc. In 1962, he graduated with honours in natural science and went on to attend Trinity Hall at Cambridge University for a PhD in cosmology.

When he turned 21, his life took a sudden tragic turn, when he was diagnosed with amyotrophic lateral sclerosis, while he was studying cosmology at the University of Cambridge. Beginning to notice issues with his health (falling, or slurring in his speech), he didn't probe into the issue until 1963, and kept these symptoms to himself. But when his father started noticing his troubled health, he asked Stephen to undergo a number of tests at a medical clinic. Subsequently, doctors alerted the Hawking family about what was ailing him: amyotrophic lateral sclerosis. In layman language, the nerves that controlled his muscles were shutting down, and doctors predicted that he would not survive for more than two and a half years.

As devastating news as it was for Hawking and his family, a few parallel incidents, however, prevented him from becoming absolutely sad and depressed. One of the things that inspired him was when Hawking was still in the hospital, there he shared a room with a boy suffering from leukemia. Looking at his neighour's predicament, Hawking later realise that his own situation seemed more sufferable. The other and the most significant motivation in his life was the fact that he was in love with Jane Wilde, a young languages undergraduate whom he met at a New Year's party in 1963, shortly before being diagnosed with ALS. They got married in 1965. His illness made him realise the value of life, and pushed him to become the famous physicist of all times. Hawking before knowing about his disease did not particularly like studies. With this eye-opening moment of fragility of his own life, he mustered all his courage and energy into his research work.

In 1974, Hawking's research transformed him from an ordinary individual to a popular name within the scientific world when he created "Hawking radiation". Despite his degenerative sickness, he had performed path-breaking work in physics and cosmology, and many of his works have aided in making science appealing to quite a number of people. Hawking had contributed his heart and soul to the realm of science, cosmology and physics, and therefore is known for his work regarding black holes and for authoring numerous popular science books. He also worked as an academician, and a teacher at several colleges, such as Caltech, Caius, Gonville, and Cambridge University. Over the years, he won several records and awards and many honours and titles for his remarkable contribution and service to the scientific arena. A section of his life story was showcased in a biographical fashion in the 2014 film *"The Theory of Everything"*, which was heartily received by the audience.

❑

Contents

LIFE SECTION

Early Life

Stephen William Hawking was born on the 8th of January, 1942 during the Second World War. His parents, Frank and Isobel belonged to the middle class. Both had studied at Oxford. At that time, they used to live in Highgate on the northern outskirts of London. It was bombed almost every night. But the University towns of Oxford and Cambridge were safe. So, they decided to have the delivery of the baby in Oxford. Till 1950, the Hawking family lived in Highgate. During this period, Stephen's two sisters, Philippa and Mary were born. Stephen was thirteen years old when his younger brother, Edward was adopted.

Stephen's parents were not rich. Frank was the grandson of a progressive farmer of Yorkshire. In the beginning of the 19th century, during the farm recession, his grandfather became bankrupt. Isobel was one of the seven children. Her father was a doctor in Glasgow. He could not afford to send any of his children to Oxford for higher education. Yet he sent his daughter there.

Frank was already studying there. He had obtained his degree in medicinal science and had specialised in it. During the

Stephen Hawking with His Sister, Mary in 1948

World War-II, he was in East Africa. To volunteer in the war, he returned to his country by ship. But instead of being recruited in the army, he was assigned to assist the doctors.

After obtaining a degree from Oxford, Isobel worked at several places. She also became an inspector in the Income Tax Department. But very soon she got fed up with the job and started working as a secretary. This change turned out to be lucky for her as she met Frank Hawking.

Hawking had a small family. He had a good collection of books. Frank and Isobel understood the importance of education. They wanted to send eleven-year-old Stephen to a reputed public school of London. Frank always felt that many of his friends, even though being less capable, had surpassed him. He believed that this was due to their affluence and higher social status. His education had suffered due to his father's poverty; he did not want this to happen in the case of his son; that is why, he wanted his son to study in a reputed school. Unfortunately, Stephen fell sick a few days before the examination for the grant of scholarship. So, he was admitted to the village's Saint Albans High School for girls (then the boys up to the age of ten years were allowed to attend the girls' school). Frank believed that here Stephen would get the same level of education as in a London school.

While Stephen was still in school, he developed interest in psychic power. While rolling the dice, Stephen and his friends would try to control them by their thoughts. Stephen heard a lecture by a learned scholar of this field, which generated revulsion against this power in his mind. The guest speaker from America told several fascinating things. He even performed an experiment. The apparent results were more or less okay, in spite of the fact that the technique was faulty. Even when the technique was fault-free and correct, the results were incorrect. Hence, Stephen concluded that psychic power is only an imagination. From then on, he firmly believed that results attained by the psychologists by controlling the senses were baseless. At that time, Stephen was only fifteen years old.

Stephen did not have much liking for sports, but he enjoyed canoe rowing even more than studies. A lot of people were present for boating in the early morning. Even though at that time, due to fog, it was very hard to do boating, yet everyone enjoyed it. Stephen also gained a lot of friends. Amongst them were several well-known members of reputed universities. His performance was appreciated in several competitions. Even though Stephen was not very successful in sports, yet it helped to develop the spirit of competition in him.

Wager

At the age of twelve, two of Stephen's friends bet with each other. One said, "Stephen will not be able achieve anything in life." The other said, "I do not agree with it." Their argument took the form of a bet. The prize was a box of chocolates for the winner of the bet.

During his youth, there was nothing exceptional about Stephen. He was intelligent but there was nothing special about

Stephen at His St. Alban Home at the Age of Twelve

it. Like other British children, he was also average. He was also not amongst the top five students of his class. But he was extremely interested in the operations of the clock and radio—he also was curious about their assembly. He used to take apart the clock and radio, but rarely was he able to put them together again. He was also not good in sports, so the friend, who thought him to be ordinary, was sure of winning the bet. The other friend had recognised the qualities overlooked by Stephen's parents and teachers. That other friend was the real winner of the box of chocolates. His feeling and belief have now been accepted by everyone. Stephen is known as one of the most intelligent scientists of the world.

At the age of nine or ten, Stephen decided to become a scientist. He thought that by learning science, he will be able to learn the reality not only about the clock or the radio, but also about all things around him. His father wanted him to become a biologist. Stephen's belief was that 'since biology was not an accurate and exact science, it was not suitable for him'. In this stream of science, he was required to examine plants and trees and study them in depth. This required good drawing skills, in which Stephen was very poor.

He was especially interested in a stream of science which enabled to understand the fundamentals of the causes and gave definite answers to the methodology. Also at that time, biology was not so much advanced. By the time he was fourteen, his slight interest in arithmetic, mathematics and physics, turned into an obsession. Initially, his father felt that Stephen's interest did not have much scope for his future. It was difficult to get any job other than that of a teacher.

At Oxford on Graduation in 1962

Eventually, it was decided that Stephen would take admission in Oxford University and study subjects like chemistry, physics and mathematics. So, at the age of seventeen, Stephen took admission in Oxford University to study natural sciences. All the students in his class were older than him. He had taken admission in the university, after serving in the army for two-three years. The initial year and half were boring for Stephen. It was not possible for him to get over the boredom of being engrossed in studies. He knew that he could leave behind his classmates even without much hard work. The first year passed listlessly, but there was a lot of change in the second year, which drew the attention of his teachers towards him. He appeared very enthusiastic and active. He got engrossed in the place. His long hair and happy disposition became his identification and made him popular. He had great interest and devotion for science.

In those days, in Oxford University, it was not very fashionable to be studious. It was assumed that if you were intelligent, then you should be able to get higher grades without much effort. If you were not intelligent, then you must live with the feeling of inferiority. Only an intelligent student could succeed in the examinations without much study. It was widely believed that putting a lot of effort and studying very hard were the signs of being stupid.

The curriculum at Oxford was accordingly prepared so that it could be completed without much hard work. The course duration was for three years, followed by an examination. Stephen used to study only for an hour in a day. So, he studied for one thousand hours in three years. He used to proudly say, "I am not proud of the practice of not working hard. But all my friends were inclined not to work hard. One advantage of my short life, on account of my sickness, made me realise that I had to achieve a lot in a short time." His teachers would say that he did not read books, would not make notes in the class, but he enjoyed finding errors in the books.

In the third year at Oxford, Stephen opted for specialisation in Cosmology. This science deals with the study of the creation of the universe and related events. Where did the universe appear from? How was it created? He raised such basic issues of this field. He applied in Cambridge University for his PhD. There he tried to get Professor Fred Hoyle to be his guide. Professor Fred informed him, "You can only join me for research, if you get first division at Oxford." To get a first division at Oxford, study and preparation for one thousand hours was not enough. But since the examination system was different, there was hope. The examination offered several questions and examples, from which the students were free to select which they want to answer. To solve them, only the basic knowledge was required. Stephen believed that instead of opting for the questions, he should opt for the examples of theoretical physics, which he could solve. As the examination neared, his self-confidence seemed to diminish. On the previous night of the examination, he could not even sleep properly due to his anxiety. His performance was also only average. The examiners called him for an oral test, to enquire about his future plans. In spite of the uncertainty, his self-confidence was praiseworthy. He replied, "If I get first division, then I will take admission in Cambridge University and if I get second division, then I shall continue at Oxford." His reply was appreciated by his friends also.

He just managed to get a first division. His guide, Dr. Robert Berman commented, "His examiners did realise the fact that Stephen was far more intelligent than them."

❑

Admission in Cambridge and Incurable Disease

In 1962, Stephen joined Trinity Hall, Cambridge. His first year was very bad. He was unable to get Dr. Fred as his guide for research. In his place, he was assigned to Dr. Dennis William Sciama.

There, his health started deteriorating. When he went home for the winter vacations, it became difficult for him to even tie his shoe laces. This change in him drew the attention of his father Frank. He took him to his family doctor. He was referred to a specialist. After examination, it became evident that Stephen was suffering from an incurable disease called 'Amyotrophic Lateral Sclerosis' (ALS). It is a serious neurological disease that affects the ability to move. The motor neurons, which send messages from the brain to the muscles, are damaged by ALS. Weakness, stammering, difficulty in swallowing are some of the initial symptoms of this disease. Gradually, as the disease progresses, all movements and speech are affected. Eventually, the patient is unable even to breathe and dies.

With Wife Jane Wilde in 1965

However, the brain is not affected till the end. For some patients, this is a boon whereas for others, it is a curse. In the last stages, the patient is given morphine injection. It is not to reduce the pain but to control his anxiety and depression.

Stephen was shocked to know that he was suffering from an incurable disease, which was drawing him closer to his death. 'Why was I am the only one affected by this disease?' In how many days will my condition become pitiable?' These were some of the questions churning in his mind. The doctor advised him to continue with his PhD, which was anyhow limping. Apart from the fact that he was suffering from the disease, he was disturbed by the thought that he may not be alive by the time the PhD was awarded to him. So, what was the point of making the effort? Such thoughts drove Stephen into depression and he started drinking excessively. According to his friends, "He would listen to Wagner's music for hours." Contradicting this, Stephen said, "It was a false propaganda that I started drinking excessively and listened to music to overcome boredom."

Even before the diagnosis of his disease, Stephen had become tired of his life. He could not focus on any work. However, one day after his return from the hospital, he suddenly felt that he could do a lot of good work, which could benefit others, even by sacrificing his life.

The doctors believed that Stephen's condition will remain stable. But the disease started intensifying. They said that he will live only for two more years. This prompted Frank to request Dr. Sciama to complete his son's research work at the earliest. But considering Stephen's restricted working ability, Dr. Sciama rejected Frank's plea stating, "Even though he may be dying, yet I will not compromise on the quality of work nor allow any shortcuts."

Two years passed, yet there was no further deterioration in Stephen's condition. He started enjoying life even more. He needed a support to move around, but his condition was stable. He was nowhere near total incapacitation or death. He was going to live, so it was necessary for him to take interest in living.

In the New Year's party of January 1963, he met a girl named Jane Wilde. She found this indifferent and whimsical person exceptional and interesting. She took a liking to his simple, amusing and pleasant nature. Hawking told her that he was studying the creation of the universe. But she was totally ignorant of this subject. They started meeting after his return from the hospital. His condition was pitiable and touching. Jane realised that Hawking had lost the will to live. She found him to be very complicated. She thought that if they unite, then a lot could be achieved. She wanted to give a new meaning to her life. Taking care of Hawking and looking after him became her aim. They fell in love and got married. They were excited that they have got a purpose in life. Hawking regained his will to live. His research work also started progressing.

Now, his thought was, 'How lucky I am! The disease has not affected my brain and intelligence, howsoever, affected my body might be. Life may not be so beautiful but it is also not so harsh. Whatever the circumstances, it is in a man's hand to live it in the best manner'. That is why theoretical science stimulated his intelligence. Looking at Hawking, one could conclude that being handicapped in our life is an ordinary matter. It is wrong even to declare him a sick person. Comparing to his physical disability versus his overall health, he could be said to be a very healthy person. This thought and message is reflected in his writing and his behaviour also. The people close to him also felt so all the time.

❑

Lively Personality

After 1960, Hawking's physical condition deteriorated again his disease aggravated and it became necessary for him to use crutches. After a few months, he could not move at all. Earlier it took him fifteen minutes to climb the stairs and reach his bed. But now all movements ceased. Hawking did not want his disease to overpower him. Using conveniences could have eased his life and would have reduced inconvenience of others. But using conveniences would have meant accepting defeat. He would frequently say, "Some would call it determination, while others obstinacy. But I have lived my life till now based on determination and obstinacy." In spite of the suffering, Hawking refused to use any aids. Jane also maintained a normal attitude towards him. This was the right thing to do. That is why her husband was able to lead life almost like a normal person.

Hawking was doing his PhD on the creation of the universe. How did it happen? Why did it happen? The key question was whether it was really created. During this time, he heard the lecture of Roger Penrose. He believed that a star after exhausting its nuclear fuel will keep getting smaller and will eventually

Stephen Boating in a Relaxed Mood

disappear. This could happen to the universe also. The thesis written by him earned the PhD degree.

In 1974, he tried to unite the Principle of Relativity and Mass Principle. Microscopic particles do not follow the regular physical laws. These particles can be created in the outer space. Their speed and form keeps on changing every moment. They are created in pairs and destructed on collision. Hawking concluded that out of the pair, one particle is drawn in the opposite direction and the other particle is thrown out. The uniting of the Principles of Relativity and Mass Principle was called the Grand Unification Theory or the Principle of Grand Unification.

He presented his 'Black Hole Explosion Principle' in a science conference, which was not understood by several scholars. Those who understood were also shaken. The chairman of the conference was a professor of London University. He was very much disturbed and he said, "Stephen, what you are saying is totally meaningless and should be thrown in the garbage bin."

Hawking published the so-called 'Garbage' in the *Nature* magazine. Within a short time, it became a topic of discussion amongst the physicists and Hawking's name became world famous. Now, Hawking was recognised as a well-known Research Scientist.

❑

Hawking's God

In the beginning of 1970s, Hawking used to go to his department in a wheelchair. It had become impossible for him to walk. His friends felt sad on his condition and would take pity on him. Even in this situation, he retained his ability to work and his jovial nature. Stephen and Jane both decided to consider the disease on a low key. It was Jane's responsibility to take care of the difficult task of looking after the growing family and her wheelchair-confined husband. She took a lot of care to ensure that the children enjoyed their childhood and her husband continued his research. She said that it was her unflinching faith in God, which made it possible.

Stephen was not a partner to her unmoving faith and belief in God. But he was not completely an unbeliever. It was difficult to discuss the creation of the universe without accepting the popular belief of existence of God—he has elaborated this idea in his book titled *A Brief History of Time*. He says that the research on creation of the universe lies on the boundary line of religion and science, but I would prefer to remain inside the limits of science. He says that he is not an unbeliever but the designation

Prof. Stephen at one of His Early Classrooms at Cambridge

of God seems like the manifestation of the laws of physics. On a small planet, we are worthless ordinary living beings. The Earth is a planet of normal stars whereas the Sun is one of the stars of millions of galaxies. Therefore, it is difficult to believe the existence of God who takes care of all big and small living beings on Earth.

Some people accept Jane's idea that Stephen's ideas on God is very limited. Lot of intelligent and practical persons have told that they have experienced the existence of God. Should their views be considered as a deliberate attempts to cheat and deceive by making use of their intelligence? Hawking's one statement is important: "If he does not exist, then there definitely must be some foreign hand." According to Jane, "Stephen's disbelief in God hurts me. I don't think his statement is correct. He seems to overlook the fact that truth obtained through mathematics is incomplete."

In the next two years, Jane developed some flexibility. She said that Stephen must have developed such thoughts on account of his condition. How could they be the same as that of other normal persons?

Legend in the World of Science

At that time, it seemed that Hawking's arrival in Cambridge University was a God's gift to it. After his appointment, Cambridge University's reputation rose quite a bit. By that time, Hawking had become a legend in the world of science. The University provided him with an equipment to turn over the pages of books and a computer terminal. He was also allotted a well-organised office room. Till 1974, Hawking could eat food with his own hands and reach his bed. But gradually the routine chores became more and more difficult to perform. His family realised that he will be unable to do anything himself. So, arrangements were made for his research assistant to stay with him.

Some people also sighted a positive outcome of Hawking's sickness. He used to spend his entire time in research, which caused lot of heartburn in his colleagues.

If Hawking was praised in front of someone from Cambridge, then he would definitely say, "The credit should really go to Jane." She left her job, did everything so that her husband could live. So, her contribution is more valuable than her husband's work. She brought up the three children and gave them a good standing. In 1970, Hawking's reputation attained the highest levels. Apart from being a strict disciplinarian, he was also known as a jolly scientist.

At the Cambridge University in 2001

It was impossible to imagine that Stephen could have attained the success or lived his life without Jane, during this period. So, it can be said that whatever other factors there might have been behind his success, Jane's sacrifice was definitely one of them. But he never acknowledged it.

In 1974, at the age of thirty-two, Hawking was appointed as the Fellow of the Royal Society (FRS). Its every member is respectfully invited and honoured. He was also required to sign in a register. The first page of this register has the signature of Sir Isaac Newton. As per the tradition, the honoured member is required to come and sign the register on the dais. Some flexibility was allowed in the case of Hawking. He could only write gradually, so he took a pretty long time to sign. During that period, there was total silence in the hall. After signing, when Hawking raised his head, there was an enthusiastic applause in the hall.

His reputation spread all over the world. He was honoured with six titles. In the field of science, he got America's highest honour, 'Albert Einstein Award' (1978). Queen Elizabeth of

United Kingdom conferred upon him the title of 'Commander of the British Empire' and allowed him to use the symbol of the title 'CBE' with his name. He was also awarded with the Wolf Prize (1988), the Prince of Asturias Award (1989), Copley Medal (2000) and the Presidential Medal of Freedom (2009).

Appointment as Lucasian Professor

In England's Cambridge town, there is a narrow pathway. It opens from below the 11th century's 'Century Church' and gradually widens ahead. At the other end of this very green pathway is the Cavendish Laboratory, which is a major centre of research in physics. Sir J.J. Thompson discovered the electron in this place; Lord Rutherford conducted experiments on the structure of the atom here. On 29th April 1980, in its Cockcroft Lecture Theatre, several scientists and the universities' respected heads got together. Above the stage, there was a two-storeyed high board and a slide projection screen. The occasion was the inaugural address of Stephen Hawking, the thirty-eight-year-old newly appointed Lucasian Professor of Mathematics. The subject of the lecture was—"Is the end in sight for the theoretical physics?" His opening statement was—yes we are very close to the end of theoretical physics—this shocked all the reputed scientists who were present there.

Stephen Hawking was on his wheelchair. One of his students was presenting the lecture on his behalf. According to many people, the appointment of Hawking to this important post was not right. At the age of twenty, he was affected by an incurable disease called 'Amyotrophic Lateral Sclerosis' (ALS), as a consequence of which all his physical movements were affected. He was shaken by his physical weakness and the threat to his life. Even though the deterioration of his condition was slow, when he was appointed as the Lucasian Professor, he could not walk, speak, eat and even lift his head. It was also difficult to understand his speech. Only people who were in close proximity

Prof. Stephen Working in His Office

to him could understand his speech. He dictated his address to his student with great difficulty. He did not consider himself handicapped, even though his family considered him so.

He was a very intelligent and active mathematician and a physicist. Some people even considered him to be second only to Einstein. Lucasian Professor was considered to be a very respected post. In the past, Sir Isaac Newton had been appointed to this post. He even had dared to declare that his research was nearing to its end at the time of assuming the post. In fact, his intelligence, courage, and patience helped him in his arduous fight.

Daily Routine in Cambridge

Professor Hawking would be in his department at eleven o'clock every morning, on his wheelchair. Outside his cabin hung a board which read 'Please be quiet, Sir is sleeping'. It projected his humorous nature as he never slept in his office. He was always occupied with people seeking appointment to meet him, discussions with other professors, meetings and seminars, etc.

His children's photo was placed on his table. Flower pots with green plants were placed in his room. There was a full-sized photo of Marilyn Monroe on his door. Everyday a nurse would be on his call; whether old or young, she would perform her responsibilities attentively and seriously. She was required to wipe his face, comb his hair, clean his glasses, take care of any emergencies, etc. His life depended on her. Yet he never seemed helpless, but always in control of his life. Being with him seems like a gift to all the nurses and students. Exactly, at one o'clock, he would leave his cabin on his wheelchair to have lunch with his colleagues. The nurse would place a napkin around his neck and feed him little by little with a spoon. After finishing his lunch, he would immediately return to his cabin. He could control the button on his wheelchair. He would drive his wheelchair pretty fast, so anyone coming from the front could collide with him. At four o'clock in the afternoon, he never missed being in the dinning hall for his tea. There he would discuss about black holes with his colleagues. Equations were written on the tea-table itself. "If they have to be to be saved, then they have to be xeroxed," he would say jokingly. During this period, he would utter only a few words, but they would be more fundamental and meaningful than anyone else's one-hour lecture. Hawking was adept at extrapolating completely new thoughts, using very few words. He was miserly with words; therefore, every word he spoke was worth consideration. He would return to his office exactly at 4:30 and would remain there till seven o'clock in the evening. Thereafter, he would attend musical events if they were being held, but only after finishing his work.

He was bound to be affected by the adoring and praiseful interviews and TV shows, almost hero-worshipping him. In this context, Hawking would say that in order for success not go to one's head, one should believe in ascetic lifestyle. During the last fifty years, he has been telling the world: "I am not an idol." But now, his image is that of a superhero. His critics have alleged that he never contradicted being called a superhero. But, why should anyone contradict?

"When people call me extraordinarily patient, I feel embarrassed." Such type of comments appears to be modesty to most people, but appears to be heroism to the critics. There is nobody who has not faced criticism. One should gracefully accept it.

Stephen Hawking's fame brought some pacification to the lives of other disabled persons. In June 1990, in Southern California University, during the assembly of disabled people, he presented some radical ideas. He stated, "Let the disabled children mix freely with the normal and healthy children of similar age. If they are isolated from childhood, when will they mix with the mainstream? This is a discriminatory policy. I am lucky that I developed this sickness during my youth. Had I developed it during childhood, then I could have never known the pleasures of life."

❑

Difficult Family Life

Till 1974, Hawking could manage to eat, go to bed, get up from bed, etc. by himself. But, gradually, it becomes more and more difficult. Seeing that he could not manage himself, Jane Hawking allowed his research assistant to stay in the house. He was responsible for helping Stephen in all the physical chores including putting him to bed.

Stephen could not play with his children. So, Jane would fill in for Stephen. She taught them to play cricket. She used to say, "If other husbands do no help their wives in household chores, their wives would get angry, but I do not get angry." Jane had assumed the complete responsibility of managing the house by herself. At the time of taking the marriage vows, she was aware of the fact that one partner would manage the house and the other partner would manage outside duties. However, during the 1970s, this dictum was changing all around. The impression that only women will manage the household affairs was weakening. Therefore, attending to household chores, living the same stereotyped life and sacrificing her own personality—accepting these things was becoming more and more difficult for her. She

Hawking with Son Tim and Wife Jane

would help out her disabled husband and continue to encourage him all the time. But she was not ready to accept that this was the end of her life. The thought that her own personality was being depleted was tormenting her. Motherhood was important to her but being confined to only looking after her children was not acceptable to her. In any case, it was difficult to stay in Cambridge.

In the university campus, Jane's sacrifice was greatly appreciated, but she was not interested in getting this kind of admiration. There was general expectation in the educated class in Cambridge to be leaders in their fields. She decided to pursue PhD in the Middle-Aged Philology (linguistics). She became a school teacher.

Hawking had three children—Robert (1967), Lucy (1970) and Timothy (1979). In 1982, Robert was fifteen years old. He used to go and play in the grounds with his brother and sister. Robert was more mature for his age. He was filled with enthusiasm,

Emotional Moments with Wife Jane

was very active and intelligent. He was not very proficient in science and was very weak in mathematics. But his progress in his subject was praiseworthy. Robert and Lucy's advancement in their studies was a matter of pride for Jane.

Stephen's theories in physics propelled him to new heights. He was also known for his discipline and jovial nature. During this period, Jane continuously felt that despite working so hard and facing so many difficulties, she was being overlooked on account of her husband's greatness and success. Every talented person feels this pain. The other family members also thought that her job was easy, her efforts and sacrifice were not

Marrying Second Wife Elaine in 1995

extraordinary. But people, who knew both of them, felt that not only Stephen's success but his life also would not have been possible without Jane. Yet, Stephen was not prepared to accept her contribution for his success. In turn, Jane never liked his mathematical discourses.

Despite the differences, both lived happily. Both were interested in classical music and used to attend the musical shows together. Both enjoyed extending their hospitality and were known for their lavish parties at home.

Till 1970, Hawking could give lectures. By the end of 1970s and early 1980s, his speech had deteriorated to such an extent that only his family members and close friends could understand it. He had to use a translator. Pronouncing each word and framing a sentence took considerable effort and time. However, each word was very meaningful and relevant.

After marriage, Jane's administrative abilities were visible. Within a short period, she took full charge over all the household chores, as well as secured a degree from London University. She also typed her husband's research thesis. Thereafter, they thought of starting a family and their first son Robert was born in May of 1967 and daughter Lucy was born in 1970.

In 1967, Stephen's doctor told him that he only had two years' life left, which he thankfully completed; thereafter two

Prof. Stephen with Family

more years passed. Seeing his little children, renewed his spirit to live. In 1980, he worked in the physics department. He used to walk around in the corridor using a cane or taking support of the walls. He would stutter in his speech.

But his courage was intact. He would raise queries and reason with the well-known scientists after their lectures. Whereas the other scientists would be spellbound by their discourses, Stephen would question them in depth and place them in difficulty. He would raise his questions with full self-confidence and nerve. During this period, he was declared to be a 'genius'. He was also honoured with the 'Albert Einstein Award'. He could not mix freely with his colleagues regardless of his jovial nature. He was constrained by his inability to respond instantly because of his physical disability. One of his colleagues commented, "Even though his behaviour was always affectionate, yet he would hesitate to invite them over for beer, to talk or just spend some time together." That is why he was considered to be different.

It is said that it is difficult to absorb extraordinary success. Is that what happened in the case of Hawking? Was his growing popularity affecting his research? Were his courage and patience coming to an end and turning into obstinacy? It is a matter of satisfaction that he was able to balance his life, but his expectations were growing. He started getting involved in several extraneous aspects of his life and most of his time was spent in such activities. It became difficult for him to say 'no' to anyone, so he started accepting all the invitations. All such activities, praises and the honours, which he awarded to others, took him further away from Jane and his children. Jane did not accompany him on most of his foreign travels. There was a perceptible change in their relationship. She had virtually stopped giving encouragement to her sick husband. She had only one thing to say to him, "You are not God." By 1990, his married life, which was going on normally, had a sudden change. They had completed their silver jubilee and were planning to celebrate it on a grand scale. But, abruptly they separated. None of them told the reason for the separation or discussed it in public. May be they had some hope of reunification. The news of their separation, however, spread all around gradually. Everyone was saddened by this news as they were considered an ideal couple.

Was Hawking's research affected by this? According to some people, physics research refreshes the brain; others believe that research done at a tender age with conviction rejuvenates. The question is whether we should apply these ideas and beliefs to a person like Hawking?

In the later part of the 1990-2000 decade, Jane Hawking's book *Music to Move the Stars* was published. She expressed her physical and mental suffocation in the book. Jane married again and Stephen married Elaine Mason. In 1980, she was his nurse. In 2006, she divorced Stephen, accusing him of torturing her. This is the story of an exceptionally talented and highly intelligent Hawking. The space is not entirely empty; the black hole is not black—he is the creator of such seemingly meaningless principles. The person, whom we pity, shows us that limit of time and space is not what is evident. Hawking can be called as the second Einstein or the second Newton to realise that the universe could be open, while initially the no boundary proposal predicted a closed universe.

❑

Vision

Even minor matters of great men attract curiosity. There are no doubts on the importance of the scientific achievements of Hawking. But this is only one aspect of his life. It is also necessary to know as to how he is as a person. There are several aspects in everyone's life. How does he appeal to his wife; as a father, which facet is important or painful to the children; how do his friends and colleagues feel about him? Each one has different feelings and experiences. It is also important to learn as to how was he in his youth and how was he during his later years. How was he during his childhood or as a student? It would be wonderful and alluring to know of the changes which occurred, after one achieves importance and respect in the society. Every person is independent and different. It is, therefore, important to see and study the human life, to understand the human mind's complexities and intricacies. As the person attains success, he moves farther away from his family and starts adoring his own personality. Others seem insignificant to him.

If this is the outlook of a common individual, then what can one say about an extraordinary person like Hawking? It would be exciting to find out. So, in this

chapter, we shall learn about the opinion of two persons close to him.

Jane Hawking, the Charming Wife

Wife Jane Hawking

Jane—who spent twenty-five years with him. In the spring oft 1990, they separated. In 1999, Jane's book *Music to Move the Stars: My Life with Stephen* was published. She has expressed her anguish and anxiety in the book. In this book of 610 pages, she has detailed the stress which she experienced and the resulting difficulties which she faced. The exertion, fatigue, and suffering she underwent while taking care of Stephen and bringing up the children, the mental struggle on account of her loneliness, and the time spent with her husband engrossed in his research—all these are described in the book. "You are inferior in intelligence to your husband"—people gave this complex to her. Her husband was an atheist, whereas Jane was a devoted Christian. She had another grouse that though Stephen had respect for her as a person, yet he had no respect for her dedication and feelings.

After the publication of Stephen's book *A Brief History of Time* in 1988, there were fresh complications. Hawking's fame grew manifold. From then on, his research colleagues and reporters ignored her. Jane stated in her book, "No one was interested in her opinion, as her husband's ideas were much more important. I started feeling inconsequential. It seemed that my existence had ceased. In fact, it was on my suggestion he wrote a popular book on cosmology of the universe. I used to constantly encourage him. However, my condition became pitiable after the popularity of the book. In 1989, Stephen started getting intimate with a nurse named 'Elaine Mason' and our relationship cooled off even more. Hawking filed an application for divorce and, in 1995, he married Elaine." Should we accept Jane's contention in the book? Stephen behaves with others as per his whims and fancies; in intelligence, no one can equal him. But, physically, he is as helpless as a small child.

The allegations of Jane are not accepted by several people. According to Stephen's Secretary, "Stephen is a good man. I used to accompany him during his foreign visits. Jane would seldom accompany him. Her behaviour was strange."

Daughter Lucy Hawking

Daughter Lucy Hawking

Stephen's daughter Lucy's thoughts are significant. Lucy was born in 1970. When her parents separated, she was 25 years old. She had written an article for *Sunday Times* about her mother, in which she wrote—"It is unlikely that there would be a woman like my mother. Even my father is a good man; however, our family went through a lot of stress due to his disability and could never overcome from it. My mother would be exhausted by her efforts of looking after him, but father was never grateful. They fell further apart on account of father's disability and his popularity. My mother loves art, music, and is a strong-willed woman. She is a spendthrift. My father is a great scientist and is committed to succeeding. They might have decided to separate on account of strong differences in their personality, interests, and mutual shortcomings."

Some more observations of Lucy are—"Books were very important in our home. I grew virtually in their company." She lays much emphasis on one aspect of Stephen—"After impediment in the speech of my father, he had great difficulty in the pronunciation of each word. When people could not understand what he was saying, he used to get livid. His anger would pain all of us. From childhood, I used to prepare breakfast for him. Even when the toasts were burnt or the tea was tepid, he used to affectionately say—'The tea is as I like it'. After my father's condition deteriorated, people would look at us with pity. I never liked it. Getting piles of mails and the ever-ringing telephone would constantly remind us of his popularity. People viewed our family as the wife and children of an extraordinary scientist. We felt that because of him we gained a lot, but at the same time, lost a lot also."

Lucy's article depicts profound love for her parents. In childhood, all fathers are the same for all children. The affection of the father towards his children is unselfish. There is no question of any give or take. The love of the mother towards her children is the same world-over, only the intensity may vary. After thirty years' stay in London, an Indian had written: "Their mothers also shed tears like our mothers. The parents' affection towards her daughter when she leaves for her in-laws house and the affection of the children towards their parents is in the blood. Because of this mystery, the sentiment of love is visible all over the world. The affection between father and daughter remains lifelong. One tends to become emotional after reading Lucy's article and it seems that their family is like ours, involved with each other."

At NASA Headquarters, while Delivering a Lecture. His Daughter Lucy is also with Him

Real Grief

One Indian Researcher, Dr. A.B. Pandit, who spent eight years in Cambridge University, doing research in chemical engineering, was there in the 1990s. He said narrating his experience, "I saw Hawking moving around on his wheelchair several times, but I did not know who he was. Some days later, I happened to meet him over dinner. I could not resist the temptation of speaking to him. It is a fact that he was a prompter of encouraging dialogue. While speaking, he had an amazing self-confidence. This left a lasting impression on me. The doubt and nervousness of talking to such an authority vanished from my mind instantly. We talked for about twenty minutes. He never uttered a single word about his disability. He was once asked, 'Which is the thing that has caused most grief to you on account of your disability? His reply was heart-breaking. He had replied, 'Due to my disability, I could not play with my children'. His ability to focus and take unbiased view of his work were the traits of his personality, which left a lasting impression on me."

❑

INTERVIEW SECTION

I had Thought of Becoming the Prime Minister

Q: Why do you think that you have been given the status of a celebrity as a scientist? Is the credit for it on account of your being disabled?

Ans. Yes, my being disabled is a consideration. People are enamoured of the fact that I am working on the great expanse of the universe in spite of my disability. I am a model of a talented disabled person or I can also say that physically I am a talented disabled person. Even though I am a disabled person, yet I am open to criticism.

Q: How do you react to all sorts of questioning by the reporters?

Ans. I do not pay too much attention to what the reporters write about me. I consider it as publicity of the media. To attract attention, a person like Einstein is required. I think it is comic to compare me with Einstein. May be they do not understand either Einstein's work or mine.

Q: How do you react to the comment: "Is it not a matter of shame that such a brilliant mind is imprisoned in such a useless body?"

Ans. I have never heard anyone say it. If anyone would have said it, I would have filed a defamation case against him.

Q: Do people express sympathy towards you on account of your disability despite your talent?

Ans. Generally, I have seen that people, who have not heard about me, treat me nicely and are helpful. I am not a sensitive person. In case they show pity towards me, it is their fault.

Q: Do people discriminate against you of being talented on account of your disability?

Ans. My colleagues do not discriminate against me in any manner on account of my disability or physical incapability except that they have to wait for me to write whatever I want to say.

Q: When was the first time you developed interest in physics and why?

Ans. I was always interested in science, like how things work. Approximately, at the age of fifteen, my attention was drawn towards physics, because, in science, this subject was most fundamental.

Q: Will you say that it is the right for a disabled person to become an astronomer?

Ans. For a disabled or a physically challenged person, it may be difficult to be an observing astronomy scientist. But it will be easy enough for him to be an astronomer because it requires mental capabilities and not physical fitness.

Q: Can the study of physics take you beyond your physical capabilities?

Ans. Most certainly, physics can take anyone beyond it, like other mental activities. As compared to the cosmos, human race is very ordinary. So, being disabled or physically incapable makes no difference.

Q: Did you wish to become a bus driver or anything else?

Ans. I never wanted to become a bus driver but I had thought of becoming the Prime Minister. Anyhow, I am happy that Tony Blair is the Prime Minister. As a profession, I like being a physicist and I think that my work is much better than his work.

Q: If some disabled or physically challenged person wants to become a physicist, what would be your advice?

Ans. I would advise a disabled or a physically challenged person to become a theoretical physicist. Of course, he must be interested in physics and must be talented.

Q: You are a talented scientist, yet do people ask questions from your personal assistant? If yes, then what would you like to say to them?

Ans. I am very happy that people ask questions from my personal assistant because I do not have the time to answer to all of them.

Q: What are your life's practical difficulties? Do you think that you lose time for your research on account of the time spent on your personal attention?

Ans. A lot of time is spent on my personal attention. Therefore, I keep myself aloof from teaching and meetings, so that I have sufficient time left for my research.

Q: How did your colleagues adjust to provide you a suitable working environment?

Ans. At present, my department in the university operates from an old printing press premises, where there is provision of a ramp. The department will soon be shifted to a new premises, which, I am sure, has been appropriately designed. My colleagues are very helpful. Like others, they behave normally with me and take care of my special needs. This is something which I like immensely.

(Personal Interview on BBC Television)

❑

I would Enjoy Travelling to the Outer Space in a Space Shuttle

On 30th December, 1999, Larry King (LK) interviewed Prof. Stephen Hawking (SH).

LK: As a Scientist, which is your most significant research?

SH: My research on big bang theory, black holes, and beginning and end of time.

LK: Were you interested in research from your early days? Were you considered a brilliant student?

SH: In childhood, children ask many questions because of their curiosity. When they grow up, they are told either that their questions are silly or children stop querying. I also kept asking 'why' and 'what'. Sometimes, I used to get the answers.

LK: Did you have any ideal or reliable guides?

SH: I did have some good teachers, but others were just regular ones. But I cannot name anyone who could be called an ideal or reliable guide.

With Pope Benedict at the Vatican City

LK: In Chicago, you had said that your greatest achievement is that you are still alive. On account of disease like ALS (Amyotrophic Lateral Sclerosis), were there any restrictions in your work?

SH: I could not perform in any field except in research on account of ALS. Research in the theoretical physics was the ideal field for me.

LK: Did you have any advantages on account of this disease? The question is a little peculiar, isn't it?

SH: I could solely focus on research on account of the disability. I was excused from giving hours of lectures and being part of different committees, if this can be called having an advantage.

LK: Who is the greatest scientist of this century?

SH: Most definitely, Albert Einstein. His theory on relativity (relationship between space and time) brought about a revolution in our understanding and beliefs. Even space and time curve on account of mass and energy.

LK: Where on Earth would you like to travel?

SH: Nowhere. I would like to travel in space in a space shuttle.

LK: Supposing you have to choose a new field for research after the year 2000, which field would you choose?

SH: I would like to conduct research in zoology.

LK: According to you which is the greatest invention?

SH: In my opinion, it is the printing press. It made communication of information and publication of research findings, faster and available to a larger audience. Knowledge was being disseminated to the next generation, both orally and through writings. There was a marked improvement in its transmission. There was faster development in scientific and technical areas. Today, printing has been replaced by Internet.

LK: Which invention of the future will change life materially?

SH: There will be many changes on account of developments in nuclear engineering. But it will take time. It is not going to happen in a hurry. There may not be any change for the next hundred years. Maybe it may happen after that.

LK: In 1988, you wrote the book titled *A Brief History of Time*. It made you extremely popular. It was translated in 30 languages and one million copies were sold.

SH: I had thought that this book should have been sold at the airport book shops. But for that it should have had the picture of a beautiful woman instead of me. It was the first book on science which became popular with the common people.

LK: Is there life on other planets?

SH: There can be primitive life on any planet which supports life. But the existence of intelligent beings seems unlikely.

LK: 'God keeps rolling the dice', is a famous remark of Einstein. What do you think about it?

SH: I think that on two accounts Einstein's remark is wrong. The heaps of research findings on black holes seem to suggest that God not only rolls the dice but also throws it at places where you cannot see it.

LK: What are your major concerns for the society?

SH: Population explosion and diseases. We have been able to eliminate the old diseases but till such time we do not become immortal, we shall continue to die. It is important we raise the life expectancy.

LK: What do you have to say about the Y2K bug?

SH: Y2K bug has been blown out of proportion. On 1st January, we shall start the count down. We may face some problems in certain areas but the world will not sink. If the ATM does not perform as expected then the universe will not come to an end.

LK: Are you happy?

SH: Yes.

(Interview on CNN)

❑

I also have Thirst for Love, Temptation and Desire

The *BBC Radio 4* show "Desert Island Discs" commenced on 29th January, 1942. It became very popular. It was telecast for 40 minutes, once a week. The country's most celebrated actors, musicians, scientists, writers, dancers and politicians were invited as chief guests and their favourite song records were played. They were also required to bring a book and a luxury item.

In the year 1992, on Navy Day, Stephen Hawking was the chief guest of the show. Sue Lawley hosted the show. The show was so amazing that it continued for more than 40 minutes.

Sue: How do you like your own life?

SH: My life is not normal but if you consider my capability, zeal, enthusiasm and courage, I think that it very much normal.

Sue: You have proved that you are complete in yourself in intelligence and mental faculties. Science keeps you busy!

SH: Basically, I have become an introvert as it is difficult for me to give lectures. From childhood, I was known for my talkativeness. To stimulate myself, I enjoyed having discussions with my family members and friends. During the discussions, the others would not participate much, but I used to like it very much as it helped me to organise my thoughts and generate new ideas.

Sue: But how do you satisfy your emotional needs?

SH: Physics is a good but a totally lifeless subject. It did not seem that I could live my life only studying physics. I am very lucky that music has become an important part of my life.

Sue: When you could not speak at all, then how did you feel?

SH: Even before my operation, my speech was slurred but as a matter of habit, my family members could still understand it. So, I was very much disappointed. However, David Mason of Cambridge Adaptive Communication fitted a Lenovo ThinkPad Tablet and a speech synthesizer to my wheelchair. It made my life much more comfortable.

Sue: Your family members say that you are extremely obstinate, have a sharp tongue, and are dictatorial. Is this true?

SH: Intelligent people have always been called obstinate. I feel that I am determined and remain steadfast on my words.

Sue: Were you always like this?

SH: I feel that I must be able to exercise control over my life. In many cases, we have seen that disabled people are dependent on others and spend their life as it is decided by others. But a healthy and strong person lives his life as he wishes.

Sue: When you were very young, a family friend had said that the Hawking family is very intelligent, clever, talented, and extremely cranky. Is it so?

SH: I don't think so. We were not at all cranky or even peculiar. In the town where we used to live, all the people, being of calm and serious nature, might have appeared to be different. My father was a researcher. He was an expert in the science of medicines. He said that I should follow his footsteps. But I could never develop interest in medicine science or zoology, because there was a lack of certainty. I wanted to do some solid research, so I opted for physics.

Sue: You definitely had good understanding of physics. In the university, the questions which used to take several days for your classmates to solve, you would solve them in a few hours. You definitely are possessed with exceptional talent, basically, you have inherent intelligence. Everyone is in agreement with this.

SH: During my time, Oxford's physics curriculum was pretty simple. Even without attending classes, it was possible to study it at home. It was not necessary to study it in-depth. Learning a few equations was enough.

Sue: After leaning about your life, I came to know that when the doctors told that you had only two more years to live, then it seemed to you as if you had been sentenced to death. Maybe, because of it, you became alert and conscious towards life.

SH: I was extremely disheartened by the doctor's diagnosis. 'Will I be able to complete my PhD?' I was disturbed by this thought. However, there was some improvement in my condition and I was able to speed up my research.

Sue: In one of the interviews, you had said that you are happier now than you were before your sickness. Is it true?

With His Students at Cambridge University

SH: Most definitely. Before developing motor neuron, I was fed up with my life. But the near-death experience made me realise the value of life. I understood that life is for living. We can achieve a lot in life. Everyone can do it. This disease is very painful for anyone. But as compared to others, I felt it much less. During that time, a woman encouraged me. I fell in love with her. Later, we married. Jane helped and took care of me immensely.

Sue: When you decided to become a father, did it shock your doctor?

SH: Yes it did. But, in fact, my father was my real doctor. He said that since my disease is not hereditary, there is no risk in my becoming a father. Jane took very good care of me and my children.

Sue: But, now you and Jane are not together?

SH: After my trachea operation, I needed 24-hours nursing care. This started affecting our relationship. So, I left her and moved to a separate flat in Cambridge.

Sue: You received several honours, awards and titles. You also occupied the respected Chair of Sir Isaac Newton. You continue to occupy the Chair of Lucasian Professor. In spite of your high standing, you decided to write a book for the non-scientists. Was it due to the fact that you required money?

SH: The main reason for writing the book *A Brief History of Time* is that I enjoyed writing it. While perusing the inventions of the last twenty-five years, I was stimulated and felt that I should inform all this to the people.

Sue: It was an excellent idea. One million copies of the book were sold and it broke all the previous records. People enthusiastically bought the book. Still the question remains as to how many people must have actually read the book?

SH: I have received mails from all over the world in which they have expressed that the book is excellent. It is not necessary that everyone read or understood the book, but the fact remains that the universe, in which we live, follows the laws of nature. We can understand those laws and discover them. On account of this book, this fact has been understood by the people.

Sue: Have you seen the serial "*Star Trek*" on TV? Did you like and enjoy it?

SH: It is a science-fiction serial. I have read many books on science fiction. I work in the field of science. I find them easy to understand but the fact remains that practical science excites and stimulates me more than science fiction. One studies the events which have occurred. Take the case of the black hole. The science-fiction writers never even dreamt of them. The research scientists had first predicted their existence. Today, we have the basis of their existence.

Sue: If you fall in a black hole, what will happen?

SH: What will happen? I will turn to spaghetti. They emit atoms and radiations. So, black holes keep altering. All these events are very exciting. But the attention of the science-fiction writers was never drawn towards them.

Sue: The radiations emitted by the black holes are called 'Hawking Radiations'. You started delving deeper into the theory of creation of the universe after this discovery.

SH: The black holes form when very massive stars collapse at the end of their lifecycle. On account of the collapse, their gravitational force multiplies several folds. Contrary to this, in the expansion of the universe, the gravitational field gets reduced. This is the fundamental difference between the two. We are outside the black hole but inside the universe. But both radiate heat.

Sue: Earlier, you used to believe in the Big Bang Theory for the creation of the universe. Today, you say that there is no beginning to the creation of the universe or its end, it exists on its own. Can we not infer from it that the creation of the universe is an event which never happened? Thus, there is no place for God or his role.

SH: You have oversimplified everything. The creation of the universe happened at the right time on account of a big bang. However, there is a virtual time which is at an angle to the real time. The creation of the universe can be explained by the laws of physics. It cannot be said that God whimsically created the universe and it is evolving whimsically. These principles do not confirm the existence of God or deny his existence. They do, however, show that he is not whimsical.

Sue: If you rule out the existence of God then how do you explain the events which cannot be explained by science?

SH: My works' findings are that the creation of the universe did not happen due to the whims of God. Then the question arises as to what was the reason for the creation of the universe? Maybe, the answer is that it was 'God's Will'.

Sue: Stephen, you are alive even thirty years after the doctor's prediction of your life expectancy. It was said that you cannot become father. Yet, you have three children. You have written an extraordinarily popular book. You have changed the faith and beliefs of many years on space and time. What other work would you like to take up before you depart from this world?

SH: My desire is to develop a principle by unifying gravitation, quantum mechanics, and other natural forces. I also particularly desire to discover what happens after a black hole collapses.

❑

I am Fascinated by All Things Connected to Life

Q: Which type of music do you like and why? Does it relax you? Name your favourite composer/band/singer/artists.

Ans. I mostly listen to classical music—Richard Wagner, Johannes Brahms, Gustav Mahler, etc., but I also like pop music.

Q: What do you like about 'Depeche Mode' (a music group)? How many of their and other shows have you heard/seen? Who was with you during Tuesday's musical evening?

Ans. Before Tuesday, I had never been to Depeche Mode's show. My son Tim is their fan and wanted to attend it. I really enjoyed it despite the fact that I was seated right in front of the speakers. My ears are still echoing. They really have a lot of energy.

Q: Science is a serious subject. But you have helped to popularise it. What other aspects of life are important to you and what are your extra-curricular activities?

Ans. I am fascinated by all things connected to life. I will not talk about my personal life. My main activities are music and history. Tim has provided me with a cherishable activity. We have attended several shows together.

(*Another Interview*)

❑

BOOK SECTION:
A BRIEF HISTORY OF TIME

The Story of the Creator of the World

In 1980, his daughter Lucy was ten years old. Money was required to admit her in a good school. Stephen decided to write a book on the creation of the universe, suitable for non-scientists to earn money. Two American publishers, namely Norton and Bantam were in the race to publish the book. Eventually, Bantam won the rights, by paying an advance of 2.5 million dollars. Discussions were held on the writing of the book, information and ideas were exchanged with the publisher. The publisher was keen that language should be straightforward and simple; there should be no mathematical equations in the book. Their sights were on the sales of the book. That is the reason why there is only one equation, namely Einstein's $E = mc^2$, in the book. Hawking had written to Bantam: "I want that the book should be displayed and sold at every bookstall on every airport; it should be in the hands of all the passengers."

While editing, Bantam suggested that he was moving very rapidly from explaining one concept to another concept in the

book. It would be very difficult for the ordinary readers to understand them. So, he should proceed very gradually from explaining one concept to the next one, and not jump. As a result, the draft was revised several times.

A Brief History of Time, as the book was titled, did wonders as soon as it was published. In England alone, 33 editions were released; the book was translated in many languages. It was on the topsellers' list for many months. Through the book, Hawking gained recognition amongst the generally educated masses. All over the world, a very large number of educated people bought the book as a status symbol. Hundreds of thousands of people read the book; it's quite possible that thousands of them might not have understood it. The cover of the book carried the picture of Hawking sitting in the wheelchair, which possibly created sympathy in the minds of the readers. World over he became a 'Hero'. The younger generation wore T-shirts carrying his photo. However, some people alleged that Hawking and the publisher tried to gain the sympathy of the readers by portraying his pitiable condition. Whatever might have been the case, the fact remains that Hawkings' attained financial stability on account of the fantastic sales of the book.

During the summer of 1985, Hawking went to CERN, Geneva in Switzerland. He contracted pneumonia there. As he could not breathe, the doctor decided to remove his wind pipe (tracheostomy operation). The doctor clarified that though it would save his life but he would never be able to speak. As a result his speech was very soft. Only people very close to him could hear/understand him and that too was going to end. What was left to live? But Jane gave permission for the operation and he started his life with renewed gusto. Now Hawking could not breathe from his nose or mouth. There was an opening at the back of his neck under the shirt collar for breathing.

To communicate there was only one alternative left for him—every word was shown to him on the board placed in front of him. If the word was correct, he would give the sign by raising his eyebrows. Word by word a sentence was formed. This was an arduous and difficult task. But Jane took it up cheerfully. She brought him back home; she believed that he will be more comfortable there. There were personal nurses at home to care for him. Now he needed twenty-four hours' assistance for his daily chores like bathing, eating, dressing, etc.

His life as a husband or father was almost over. Jane somehow felt that his end was near. She tried to secure aid from America. She was able to secure 50 thousand pounds of aid for the payment of the salaries of the nurses every year from an American Institution (trust). Another institution provided him with a computer. It became easier for him to find the desired words on the screen of the computer. He could operate it with his fingers (which was not always possible) or could activate a switch by the movement of his head or eyes.

Hawking trained himself rigorously in the use of the computer, got used to it and was able to achieve a speed of ten words per minute. The computer's memory contained fifty thousand words. He would prepare a sentence assembling words. The sentence could be saved at the bottom of the screen. The sentence was then fed to the speech synthesizer. Hawking would thus prepare his lecture and save it on the disc. He was able to show each sentence on a wall-mounted screen using a projector with voice also. The voice is not of Hawking or a robot. Even though the voice has British accent, it is of an East Indian through a machine. Can we feed tones and human emotions in the voice? Initially, we might feel the necessity of the refinements but later one gets used to it. Hawking's jovial nature is still alive. It is indeed amazing that when a smile appears on Hawking's face, there is no evidence of the kind of physical difficulty and pain which he is facing. He tells everyone who comes to meet him, "I have everything, please do not be concerned." He is also satisfied with the operation of the computer. He frequently says, "I can now talk to everyone." Then one realises of the grit and determination which he possesses. Hawking likes to travel. He keeps travelling within and outside the country.

Articles in Newspapers and Magazines

After the publication of his book, there were exhaustive articles on Hawking and his disease, in newspapers and magazines all over the world. "How Patiently a Physicist has Read the Mind of God" — articles with many such headlines were published. Many people came to meet and interview him. He was declared a 'Hero'. He was considered a role model for the society. In one of the interviews, his sons had called him—"Obstinate and grumpy. Once he gets an idea fixated in his mind, then he keeps chasing it, irrespective of the consequences. But this obstinacy and grumpiness is necessary, it keeps him alive and gives him strength."

Hawking's life was a success on account of his amazing optimism and determination. Earlier, only his family was concerned and had the responsibility of looking after him. Later, all the scientists of the world were concerned for his welfare. He showed to the thousands of other disabled people how life can be made pleasant regardless of acute difficulties and having acute physical disability. He used to say, "I am not a leader but a simple soul."

If one overlooks his disease, then Hawking was a very lucky person. Very few people are so intelligent few people have such fine children and very few people get a completely dedicated wife like Jane. Jane says, "Had my husband been a teacher, we would have never got the aid of fifty thousand pounds. He would still be lying in a nursing home, away from home."

There was negative criticism also to his affluent-celebrated life. According to some critics, he would never have got such popularity for a book based solely on research, had he been healthy. He capitalised on his pitiable condition by putting his photo showing him sitting in a wheelchair, on the cover page of his book. But Hawking never agreed with this criticism. It is a fact that Hawking is known for his scientific discoveries, as well as his extraordinary patience. His life turned out to be worth living by a combination of superior intelligence, extraordinary patience and matchless courage. He overcame his adverse circumstances and made his life worth living by sheer hard work. He motivated hundreds and thousands of people by it. He taught and showed that even in the worst crisis, life could be made worth living.

❑

Stephen Hawking: A Hero

In the spring of 1988, the book was distributed to the book-stalls in America. The hard cover edition was priced at $ 14.99, there was no paperback edition. The book was launched at the Rockefeller Centre in New York. The event continued throughout the day. He was meeting every visitor sitting in his wheelchair. In the evening, when the event concluded, Hawking was as much fatigued as he was happy. There was a get-together in the evening by the side of the river. Hawking was moving so fast on his wheelchair that it made Jane fear all the time that he might fall in the river. Hawking was impressed and buoyant by the lavishness of the function.

Initially, Bantam Books did not advertise and the book was not placed in vantage locations in the stores. Within a few days of the launch, there was a crisis. An editor of Bantam Books, while casually editing the book, found a mistake in the book. Two pictures had been printed at the wrong place in the book.

In all, forty thousand books were distributed. The managers of all the stores were contacted over phone, told about the mistake and requested to return the books. Every store replied, "It is not possible as all the books have been sold."

Glorified Prof. Hawking: Some of His Statues at Stephen's Office

This was a pleasant shock for Bantam Books. Sale of forty thousand copies in 2-3 days was unexpected. Bantam's editorial board was very smart. They realised the book's great potential. The mistake was corrected and immediately new prints were sent to the stores.

The review of the book was first published in *Time* Monthly Magazine. Based on the Time review, favourable reviews were published, in other magazines and papers, all over America. Within a few weeks, the book was on the bestsellers' list. Not only the book but a full-sized poster of Hawking was displayed on the store frontage.

By the end of summer of 1988, that is, in approximately four months, the book was a topseller. Five hundred thousand copies were already sold. Stephen Hawking attained wide popularity as a scientist. Young and old, all were proudly wearing shirts with Hawking's photo prints on them.

In June of 1988, the book was published in England and it got the same response as in America. All the copies of the book, which were distributed in London, were sold within a week. It was hard to get fresh stocks. By 1991, twenty editions of the book had been brought out. Every month, on an average, five thousand copies were being sold. One storekeeper remarked, "This book is being sold as if it was a religious book." The reviews in World Science and Research Magazine, *Nature and Daily Mail* were also favourable. Hawking's popularity increased so much that he was deciding himself which reporter he will meet. He felt that the general public should be informed about the book through radio. He desired that the book should be read by carpenters, plumbers, electricians, etc. He also wanted that the interest of reading the book must also be developed in doctors, engineers, teachers of science, students, etc. "My book has got the kind of popularity which a well-known musician gets. So, I am very happy." Science has a very important role to play in the lives of the new generation. So, he felt that they all must have some information about it.

By 1998, this book broke all the sales records. Hawking's popularity also touched a new high. People would stop him on the way and express their desire to talk to him. The editor of Nature had written that he was concerned about the popularity of science in the society. Hawking wanted to tell him that, in America alone, six hundred thousand copies of the book were sold. Hawking's desire that the book should become popular in the masses had been fulfilled. A science professor, who was getting his car washed at a garage, was asked by an employee there, "Do you know Professor Hawking? He is my Hero."

"What is the secret of the extraordinary popularity of this book? That six hundred thousand copies of this book priced at $ 14.99 were sold in America alone; for three years continuously it remained on the topselling books' list. Like the Creator's mysteries are miraculous and strange, similarly this book's popularity is mysterious. Anyone who explains this mystery will be rewarded by me." This declaration was made by Bernard in his article in *Time* magazine.

There were several responses.

Stephen Hawking's mother, Isobel Hawking's reply is very important. She writes: "One enjoys reading the book. Concepts are difficult but the language is simple. The book is not hollow; it does not consider the reader to be inferior or has taunted him. Hawking wishes that his concepts would be understood by any curious reader. He was able to defeat his disability by this book, which is one of the reasons of his popularity. It is true that I could not understand the book but still I read it till the last page."

Hawking's colleagues and friends have different opinions about the book. Some liked the book, others did not like it. By giving the full life history and photos of Galileo, Newton and Einstein, what did he attain or what did he want to achieve? Is it possible that the writer wanted to be sarcastic? He truthfully replied, "Yes, they had that much capability."

Renowned Russian scientist, Andre Levchenko has narrated an exciting experience:

A passenger sitting next to me in an airplane was reading *A Brief History of Time*.

I asked him, "How is the book?"

"It is interesting and extremely touching."

"I have also read the book. But I could not understand it at all."

He did not reply for some time, so I asked him, "Are you a scientist?"

"No, I am a businessman."

"Oh! Is that so?"

Then he placed the book in his lap and said, "I can explain it to you."

Even a businessman was eager to explain the concepts of creation of the universe, black holes and time travel to a renowned Russian Scientist, Andre Levchenko.

This is an incomparable example of the popularity of the book.

❑

A Brief History of Time: Summary

A Brief History of Time is a historic book of StephenHawking. In this book, Hawking has discussed several aspects of physics.

Chapter 1: Our Picture of the Universe

In this chapter, Hawking talks about the history of physics. He talks about the ideas of philosophers such as Aristotle and Ptolemy. Aristotle, unlike many other people of his time, thought that the Earth was round. He also thought that the Sun and stars went around the Earth. Ptolemy had also worked out how the Sun, planets and stars were located in the universe. He made a planetary model that described Aristotle's thinking. Today, it is known that the opposite is true; the Earth goes around the Sun. Aristotle/Ptolemy's ideas about the location of the planets, stars and Sun were proved wrong in 1609. The person who first thought of the idea about the Earth going around the Sun was Nicolaus Copernicus. Galileo Galilei and Johannes Kepler, two other scientists, helped to prove that Copernicus's idea was right. They looked at how the moons of some planets moved in the sky, and they used this to prove Copernicus right. Isaac Newton also wrote a book about gravity, which helped to prove that Copernicus's idea was right.

Chapter 2: Space and Time

In this chapter, Stephen Hawking talks about space and time. He describes the motion of planets moving around the Sun and how gravity works between the planets and the Sun. He also talks about the ideas of absolute rest and absolute position. These ideas are about the thought that events stay in place over a period of time. These ideas were proved wrong by Newton's laws of gravity. The idea of 'absolute rest' did not work when objects move very fast, i.e., at the speed of light.

The speed of light was found out in 1676 by the Danish astronomer, Ole Christensen Rømer. The speed of light was found to be very fast, but still it was finite. However, scientists found a problem when they tried to say that light always travelled at the same speed. The scientists created a new idea, called the *ether*, which tried to explain light's speed.

Einstein said that time was not absolute or always the same. He said that the idea of the *ether* was not needed, if the idea of 'absolute time' (or time that is always the same) was dropped. Einstein's idea was also the same as Henry Poincare's idea. Einstein called it the 'theory of relativity'.

Stephen Hawking then talks about light. He says that events can be described by 'light cones'. The top of the light cone tells where the light from the event will travel. The bottom tells where the light was in the past. The center of the light cone is the event. Besides light cones, Stephen Hawking also talks about how light can be bend. When light goes past a big object, like a star, the light changes the direction because the star has a lot of gravity.

After talking about light, Stephen Hawking talks about time in Einstein's theory of relativity. One prediction that Einstein's theory makes is that time will go slower when something is close to large objects, like the Earth. However, when something is farther away from the large object, time will go by faster. Stephen Hawking used the idea of twins, each living at two different places to describe his idea. If one of the twins went to live at a high place (on a mountain), and another one went to live at a lower place (near the sea), the one who went to live on the mountain would be a little bit older than the one who went to live at the sea.

Chapter 3: The Expanding Universe

Stephen Hawking talks about the expanding universe. This means he believes that the universe is expanding. One of the things he uses to explain his idea is the Doppler's effect. The Doppler's effect happens when something moves towards or away from another object. There are two types of things that happen in Doppler's effect—red shifting and blue shifting. Red shifting happens when something is moving away from us. This is due to the increase in the wavelength of the visible light reaching us, and the decreasing of frequency, which shifts the visible light towards the red/infrared end of the electromagnetic spectrum. Red shift is linked to the belief that the universe is expanding as the wavelength of the light is increasing, almost as if stretched as planets and galaxies move away from us, which shares similarities to that of the Doppler's effect, involving sound waves. Blue shifting happens when something is moving towards us, the opposite process of red shift, in which the wavelength decreases and frequency increases, shifting the light towards the blue end of the spectrum. A scientist named Edwin Hubble found that many stars are red shifted and are moving away from us. Stephen Hawking uses the Doppler's effect to explain that the universe is getting bigger. The beginning of the universe is thought to have happened through something called the Big Bang. The Big Bang was a very big explosion that created the universe.

Chapter 4: The Uncertainty Principle

The uncertainty principle says that the speed and the position (or where something is) of a particle cannot be found at the same time. To find where a particle is, the scientists throw light at the particle. If a high frequency light is used, the light can find the position more accurately but the particle's speed will be unknown (because the light will change the speed of the particle). If a lower frequency light is used, the light can find the speed more accurately but the particle's position will be unknown. The uncertainty principle disproved the idea of a theory that was deterministic, or something that would predict everything in the future.

How light behaves is also talked about more in this chapter. Some theories say that light acts like particles, even though it really is made of waves; one theory that says this is Planck's Quantum theory. A different theory also says that light waves also act like particles; a theory that says this is Heisenberg's Uncertainty Principle. Light's interference causes many colours to appear. Light waves have crests and troughs. The highest point of a wave is the crest, and the lowest part of the wave is a trough. Sometimes more than one of these waves can interfere with each other—the crests and the troughs line up. This is called 'light's interference'. When light waves interfere with each other, this can make many colours. An example of this is the colours in soap bubbles.

Chapter 5: Elementary Particles and the Forces of Nature

Quarks and other elementary particles (very small things) are discussed in this chapter.

Quarks are very small particles that make up everything we see (matter). There are six different "flavours" of quarks: the up quark, down quark, strange quark, charm quark, bottom quark, and top quark. Quarks also have three "colours": red, green and blue. There are also anti-quarks, which are the opposites of the regular quarks. In total, there are 18 different types of regular quarks, and 18 different types of anti-quarks. Quarks are known as the "building blocks of matter" because they are the smallest thing that makes up all the matter in the universe.

All particles (for example, the quarks) have something called 'spin'. The spin of a particle shows us what a particle looks like from different directions. A particle of spin 1 looks different in every direction, unless the particle is spun completely around (spun 360 degrees). Stephen Hawking's example of a particle of spin 1 is an arrow. A particle of spin 2, needs to be turned around half way (or 180 degrees), to look the same. The example given in the book is of a double-headed arrow. There are two groups of particles in the universe: particles with a spin of 1/2, and particles with a spin of 0, 1, or 2. All of these particles follow 'Pauli's Exclusion Principle'. Pauli's exclusion principle says that particles cannot be in the same place or have the same speed. If Pauli's exclusion principle did not exist, then everything in the universe would look the same, like a roughly uniform and dense soup.

A proton is made up of three quarks. All the quarks are of different colours because of 'confinement'. Particles with a spin of 0, 1 or 2 move force from one particle to another. Some examples of these particles are 'virtual gravitons' and 'virtual photons'. Virtual gravitons have a spin of 2 and they represent the force of gravity. This means that when gravity affects two things, gravitons move to and from the two things. Virtual photons have a spin of 1 and represent electromagnetic forces (or the force that holds atoms together).

Besides the force of gravity and the electromagnetic forces, there are weak and strong nuclear forces. Weak nuclear forces are the forces that cause radioactivity when matter emits energy. Weak nuclear force works on particles with a spin of 1 or 2. Strong nuclear forces are forces that keep the quarks in a neutron and a proton together, and keeps the protons and neutrons together in an atom. The particle that carries the strong nuclear force is thought to be a 'gluon'. The gluon is a particle with a spin of 1. The gluon holds together quarks to form protons and neutrons. However, the gluon only holds together quarks that are of three different colours. This means the end products have no colour. This is called 'confinement'.

Some scientists have tried to make a theory that combines the electromagnetic force, the weak nuclear force, and the strong nuclear force. This theory is called a 'grand unified theory' (or a GUT). This theory tries to explain these forces in one big unified way.

Chapter 6: Black Holes

Black holes are discussed in this chapter. Black holes are stars that have collapsed into one very small point. This small point is called a 'singularity'. Black hole sucks things into its centre because its gravity is very strong. Some of the things it can suck in are light and stars. Only very large stars called 'supergiants' are big enough to become a black hole. The star must be one-and-a-half times the mass of the Sun or larger to turn into a black hole. This number is called the 'Chandrasekhar limit'. If the mass of a star is less than the Chandrasekhar limit, it will not turn into a black hole; instead, it will turn into a different, smaller type of star. The boundary of the black hole is called the 'event horizon'. If something is in the event horizon, it will never escape the black hole.

Black holes can be shaped differently. Some black holes are perfectly spherical—like a ball. Other black holes bulge in the middle. Black holes will be spherical if they do not rotate. Black holes will bulge in the middle if they rotate.

Black holes are difficult to find because they do not let out any light. They can be found when black holes suck in other stars. When black holes suck in other stars, the black hole lets out X-rays, which can be seen by telescopes.

Stephen Hawking talks about his bet with another scientist, Kip Thorne. Stephen Hawking bet that black holes did not exist, because he did not want his work on black holes to be wasted. He lost the bet.

Chapter 7: Black Holes aren't so Black

This chapter explains more about black holes. Stephen Hawking realised that the event horizon of a black hole could only get bigger, not smaller. The area of the event horizon of a black hole gets bigger whenever something falls into the black hole. He also realised that when two black holes combine, the size of the new event horizon is greater than or equal to the sum of the event horizons of the two other black holes. This means that a black hole's event horizon can never get smaller.

Disorder, also known as 'entropy', is related to black holes. There is a scientific law that has to do with entropy. This law is called the 'second law of thermodynamics', and it says that entropy (or disorder) will always increase in an isolated system (for example, the universe). The relation between the amount of entropy in a black hole and the size of the black hole's event horizon was first thought of by Jacob Bekenstein, a research student and proven by Stephen Hawking. Stephen Hawking's calculations said that black holes emit radiation. This was strange, because it was already said that nothing can escape from a black hole's event horizon.

This problem was solved when the idea of pairs of 'virtual particles' was thought of. One of the pair of particles would fall into the black hole, and the other would escape. This would look like the black hole was emitting particles. This idea seemed strange at first, but many people accepted it after a while.

Chapter 8: The Origin and Fate of the Universe

How the universe started and how it might end is talked about in this chapter. Most scientists believe that the universe started in an explosion called the Big Bang. The model for this is called the 'hot big bang model'. When the universe starts getting bigger, the things inside it also begin to get cooler. When the universe was first beginning, it was infinitely hot. The temperature of the universe cooled and the things inside the universe began to clump together.

Stephen Hawking also talks about how the universe could have been. For example, if the universe formed and then collapsed quickly, there would not be enough time for life to form. Another example would be a universe that expanded too quickly. If a universe expanded too quickly, it would become almost empty. The idea of many universes is called the 'anthropic principle'.

Inflationary models are also discussed in this chapter, and so is the idea of a theory that unifies quantum mechanics and gravity.

Each particle has many histories. This idea is known as 'Feynman's theory' of sum over histories. A theory that unifies quantum mechanics and gravity should have Feynman's theory in it. To find the chance that a particle will pass through a point, the waves of each particle need to be added up. These waves happen in imaginary time. Imaginary numbers, when multiplied by themselves, make a negative number.

Chapter 9: The Arrow of Time

When one tried to unify gravity with quantum mechanics, one had to introduce the idea of "imaginary" time. Imaginary time is indistinguishable from directions in space. If one can go north, one can turn around and head south; equally, if one can go forward in imaginary time, one ought to be able to turn round and go backward. This means that there can be no important difference between the forward and backward directions of imaginary time.

On the other hand, when one looks at 'real' time, there is a very big difference between the forward and backward directions, as we all know. Where does this difference between the past and the future come from? Why do we remember the past but not the future?

Disorder tends to increase with time, because we measure time in the direction in which disorder increases.

Man has made tremendous progress but, as compared to the rapidly expanding disordered universe, he is still a pygmy.

Chapter 10: Wormholes and Time Travel

As the name suggests, a wormhole is a thin tube of space-time which can connect two nearly flat regions far apart. Thus, one could imagine that one could create or find a wormhole in space through which we could travel to another galaxy or travel to the past.

Wormholes were first described in 1935 by Einstein and Nathan Rosen, in a research paper in which the wormholes were called 'bridges'.

Hawking says that in future we may become so advanced in science and technology that we eventually manage to build a time machine. It is also possible that time-space alters so much that it may be possible to travel in the past.

Chapter 11: The Unification of Physics

In this chapter, it has been explained that it would be very difficult to develop a completely unified theory of everything in the universe, all at one go. So, instead partial theories, that cover a limited range of effects, are being developed. They either ignore other effects or approximate them by certain numbers.

Also in this chapter, questions have raised that if there are other dimensions, then why can't we see them? Why can we see only three space-dimensions and one time-dimension? The suggestion is that the other dimensions are curved up into space of very minute size, something like 10 to the power of 30th part of an inch. It is so small that we cannot notice it; we see only three space-dimensions and one time-dimension, in which the space-time is fairly flat.

Imagine looking at an orange from a close distance, you notice the curvature. But if you see it from a distance, then it appears flat. So, it is with space-time, on a very small-scale, it is either ten or twenty-six dimensions and highly curved, but on bigger scales, you don't see the curvature or the extra dimensions.

As has been explained, normally there are four dimensions. Maybe only in such a boundary, it is possible for complicated creatures like us to survive. Presumably, God considered everything before he created the universe. Can God make a stone so heavy that he can't lift it?

Chapter 12: Conclusion

Einstein once asked the question, "How much choice did God have in creating the universe?"

Even if there is only one possible unified theory, it is just a set of rules and equations. What is it that breathes fire into the equations and makes a universe for them to describe?

Why does the universe go to all the bother of existing? Is the unified theory so compelling that it brings about its own existence? Or does it need a creator, and, if so, does he have any other effect on the universe? And who created him?

However, if we do discover a complete theory, it should in time be understandable in broad principle by everyone, not just a few scientists. Then we all, philosophers, scientists, and just ordinary people, shall be able to take part in the discussion of the question as to why it is that we and the universe exist. If we find the answer to that, it would be the ultimate triumph of human race—for then we would know the mind of God.

Other Leading Books

- Singularities in Collapsing Stars and Expanding Universes
- The Nature of Space and Time
- The Large Scale Structure of Space-Time
- The Large, the Small, and the Human Mind
- Hawking on the Big Bang and Black Holes
- God Created the Integers

Popular Books

- A Brief History of Time
- Black Holes and Baby Universes and Other Essays
- The Universe in a Nutshell
- On the Shoulders of Giants

Children's Books

- George's Secret Key to the Universe
- George's Cosmic Treasure Hunt

Films and Serials

- A Brief History of Time (Film)
- Stephen Hawking's Universe (Documentary)
- Beyond the Horizon (Film)
- Masters of Science Fiction (Television series)
- Stephen Hawking: Master of the Universe (Television series)

❑

LECTURES/EXPLANATIONS/ WRITINGS SECTION

Universe and Life

How was life form created in the universe and the development of intelligent life—has been explained. We call the human beings intelligent, but if we study the history, it becomes apparent that the human behaviour has mostly been stupid. There are two questions. The first question is, whether there is possibility of life anywhere else in the universe? Second question is, how will life develop in the future?

Common experience tells us that with time things get more chaotic and disordered. This experience has been transformed into a law called the Second Law of Thermodynamics. According to this law, the universe's Disorder or Entropy always increases with time. This law is applicable only to the total amount of disorder.

In the living world when the order in a body increases, then the disorder in the surrounding environment increases even more. One can consider life to be an ordered system that can sustain itself against the tendency to disorder and reproduce itself. This means that this system can create an independent system like itself.

Explosion in the Galaxy

Humans, animals and birds mate and produce their own independent offsprings. In order to achieve this, the system must convert energy into some ordered form like food, to some disordered form like heat. Thus, the system obeys the second law of thermodynamics that the total amount of disorder increases, while simultaneously increasing the order in itself and its offspring. A living being has two elements: a set of instructions which tells how to sustain and reproduce itself and a mechanism to carry out the instructions. In biology, these two elements are called genes and metabolism.

Beginning of Life

Life, as we know it, is made up of chains of carbon atoms, along with nitrogen and phosphorus atoms. The fact that our universe is a marvel and our life in it is so finely tuned, apparently seems to suggest that the universe was specially designed to produce the human race.

When the universe began 15 billion years ago, it was unimaginably hot. Immediately after the Big Bang, the temperature must have fallen to a billion degrees, still a hundred times the temperature of the Sun. As the universe expanded, it must have cooled further. Anyhow, all matter would have been in its very basic particle form of protons and neutrons. Possibly, their numbers would have been equal. However, at this temperature, the neutrons will start to decay into more protons. Other neutrons must have collided with protons, stuck together to form the next simplest element, helium, whose nucleus consists of two protons and two neutrons. But no heavier elements like carbon or oxygen would have been formed in the early universe. Anyway, it was far too hot for atoms to combine into molecules.

The universe continued to expand and cool. Some regions must have had higher densities than others. In such regions, the expansion would slow down due to gravitational attraction and eventually stop. Consequently, they would collapse to form galaxies and stars. This could have taken about two billion years after the Big Bang. Some of stars would have been heavier and hotter than the Sun. They would have burnt their hydrogen and helium into heavier elements like carbon, oxygen and iron. This process could have taken about a few hundred million years.

Our solar system was formed about four-and-a-half billion years ago, that is, approximately ten billion years after the Big Bang, from gas contaminated with remains of the earlier stars. Formation of the Earth happened out of heavier elements like carbon and oxygen. It is not known how, but some of these atoms were arranged in the form of molecules of DNA (the building blocks of life). Its structure in the form of a double helix was discovered by two scientists, Crick and Watson in Cambridge. Linking the two chains in the helix are two pairs of nucleic acids—adenine (A) with thiamine (T) and guanine (G) with cytosine (C), that is AT and GC.

An adenine on one chain is always matched with a thiamine on the other chain, and a guanine with a cytosine. Thus, the sequence of nucleic acids on one chain defines a unique, complimentary sequence, on the other chain. The two chains can then separate and each act as templates to build further chains. Thus, DNA molecules can reproduce the genetic information, coded in their sequences of nucleic acids.

Can there be DNA like molecules in another solar system? We can expect they could exist in few galaxies. But they would be very far away from the centre of the respective galaxies. It is not surprising that life form developed on Earth. It was made possible by the supportive atmosphere and necessary elements.

Carbon dating of fossils found on Earth suggests that there was some form of life on Earth about three-and-a-half billion years ago. That is only 500 million years after the Earth became stable and cooled enough for life to develop. That life developed so early suggests that it was spontaneous and conditions were conducive. Maybe there was some simpler structure of DNA. One possibility is RNA. It is like DNA but without the double helix structure. Short lengths of RNA could reproduce themselves like DNA and could eventually build up to become DNA.

One cannot make nucleic acids in the laboratory from non-living material, let alone RNA. But given 500 million years, and oceans covering most of the Earth, there might be a reasonable probability of RNA, being made by chance.

The process of biological evolution was very slow at first. It took two-and-a-half billion years to evolve from the earliest cells to multi-cell animals. It took another billion years to evolve through fish and reptiles to mammals. But then evolution seems to have speeded up. It only took about a hundred million years to develop from the early mammals to humans. The reason is, fish possess most of the important human organs. In case of mammals, they possess essentially all the human organs. All

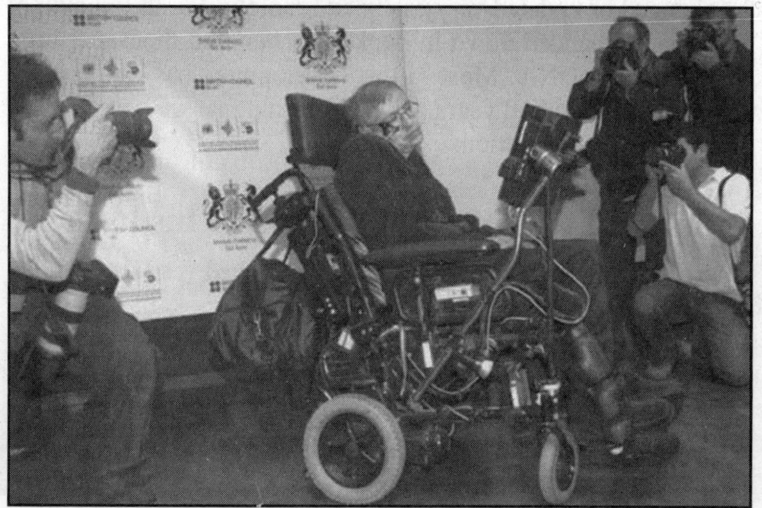

Prof. Hawking Surrounded by Photographers during His Israel Visit

that was required to evolve from early mammals, like lemurs, to humans, was minor improvements.

Human Evolution

There was an important evolution in humans, as important as the development of DNA. The development of spoken language and then, more importantly, written language. Information could be passed on from generation to generation, other than genetically, through DNA. Even though in ten thousand years there has been no detectable change in human DNA, in spite of the significant biological evolution.

The DNA in human beings contains about three billion nucleic acids. Most of the information coded in this sequence is redundant or inactive. The total amount of useful information in our genes is approximately one hundred million bits. One bit of information is the answer to a yes/no question. In contrast, a paperback novel contains two million bits of information. So a library with five million books will contain ten trillion (ten thousand billion) bits of information. This information can also be changed or updated very easily and rapidly. So, the amount of information handed down in books is a hundred thousand times as much as in DNA. Most of this development has happened in the last three hundred years. This has meant that we have entered a new phase of evolution.

Limits of Learning and Aggressive Instincts

There was a man in the 18th century who had read every book written. Today, if one tries to read every book in a national library, it will take him about 15,000 years. No one person can master all knowledge. They will only be able to specialise in limited fields. This is likely to be a major limitation in the future.

Anyhow, we and our future generations will be on a higher level of learning. This might pose a danger. We still have the instincts, and, in particular, the aggressive impulses that we had in cave man days. This could lead to destruction of much of the human race and life on Earth—a nuclear war, genetic warfare or instability in the greenhouse effect.

We have already entered into a new phase, which might be called self-designed evolution or genetic engineering. It will be possible to change and improve our DNA. At first, these changes will be confined to the repair of genetic defects, like cystic fibrosis, and muscular dystrophy. These are controlled by single genes, and so are fairly easy to identify and correct.

Other qualities such as intelligence are probably controlled by a larger number of genes. It will be much more difficult to find them, and work out the relations between them. Nevertheless, it is certain that during the next century, people will discover how to modify both intelligence, and instincts like aggression. Once such superhumans appear, there are going to be major problems, with the normal humans, who won't be able to compete. Presumably, they will die out, or become unimportant.

If this race manages to redesign itself, to reduce or eliminate the risk of self-destruction, it will probably spread out, and colonise other planets and stars. However, long distance space travel will be difficult for chemically-based life forms, like DNA. The natural lifetime for such beings is short as compared to the travel time.

❑

Life on Other Planets

We are searching the galaxy for some alien form of life on other planets. If the argument about the time scale for the appearance of life on Earth is correct, there ought to be many other stars, whose planets may support life. These planets might have been created billions of years before Earth was created. If so, then why has the Earth not been visited by mechanical or biological forms of life? If there would have been any kind of visits, they would not have been shrouded in mysterious sightings of UFOs. The suggestions that these UFOs were manned by aliens is much more far-fetched. If they were true, they would have been more obvious and may not have been necessarily pleasant.

Is there any explanation as to why we have not been visited by aliens? Maybe Earth was the only planet where life appeared spontaneously and further evolved into intelligent beings. Another possibility is that, in other places, only self-reproducing systems like single-cells were formed, but that most of these forms of life did not evolve intelligence. The Anthropic Principle suggests that evolution is a random process with evolution of intelligence

UFO (A Myth or Reality)

as only one of the large number of possible outcomes. Further intelligence possibly has short-term survival value. After all, we have been in existence for an infinitesimally small time, if we compare it to the time scales of the universe. Bacteria and other single cell organisms will survive even if all other forms of life on Earth are wiped out, by our actions or other events like comet or asteroid collisions.

One explanation for the extinction of dinosaure is that a smaller body collided with Earth 70 million years ago. Only a few small early mammals survived. Thereafter, it has been a collision-free period and that is why intelligence survived. Planets in other galaxies might have not been so lucky.

❑

Arrow of Time

All principles tell us that the universe is not indestructible. It was created 15 billion years ago. The discovery of the creation of the universe and the related events are considered extraordinary. But we cannot say with certainty whether it has an end or not. The lifespan of the universe is far greater than the human lifespan. That is why, it was our belief that the universe is stable. Many people were disturbed by the fact that there was a beginning of the universe. Because, it would be concluded that the universe was created by a supernatural power. Their belief was that the universe and humans were there from time eternity. They would keep on harping that on account of floods and other natural calamities, man could not develop and remained in his preliminary state.

During the 19th century and 20th century, the dispute whether there is a beginning of the Earth or not remained open. Religious proponents and philosophers also continued to debate. The theory that the universe is indestructible defies the second law of thermodynamics. Several contradictions arise due to it.

According to this law, the disorder of the universe increases continuously with time. Universe must have been created because from that moment the disorder started increasing.

It is certain that the universe is not stable; we can also say that the galaxies are gradually expanding, which means that, in the past, they were closer. Consider the two expanding galaxies. If we track their paths, ignoring gravity, then they will be in a straight line. Now if we retrace their tracks, going back to zero time, that is about 20 billion years ago, then these tracks will merge. But, in reality, the effect of gravity will bring them closer and their path will be curved instead of being straight. It is still possible that 20 billion years in the past there will be zero difference. At that time, due to the Big Bang, all the elements of the created universe would have stuck together. At that point, the density would have been infinite. This state is called Singularity. No laws of physics are applicable on it, which means that post Big Bang, universe is not dependent on its prior state.

Since the prior state is not relevant, we shall ignore it while formulating our principles. The Big Bang phenomenon is not explicitly clear to us, as there are no yardsticks to gauge it.

Till the beginning of the 20th century, people believed in an absolute time. Every event was tied to a specific time and it occurred at that time only. All good clocks would show the same time interval between two events. However, the discovery that the speed of light was the same to every observer, irrespective of how he was moving, led to the theory of relativity and idea of time being absolute was abandoned.

In order to unify gravity with quantum mechanics, the idea of 'imaginary' time had to be introduced. Imaginary time is indistinguishable from directions in space. In imaginary time, if one heads towards north, then he can turn around and head south. Similarly, if one is going forward, then he can turn around and go backwards. That is, direction is irrelevant in imaginary time.

Whereas in real time, there is a major difference between forward and backward directions. The laws of science are the same for the past and the future. Then where does this difference between the past and the future come from? Why do we remember the past but not the future?

To understand the difference between the forward and backward directions of real time, imagine a porcelain cup which falls off a table and breaks into pieces on the floor. If you film this event, then you can easily tell if it is being run forward or backward. The forward motion will show the breaking of the cup, whereas the backward motion will show its reassembling.

The second law of thermodynamics forbids the event of reassembling of the cup happening. It says that in any closed system, the disorder or entropy always increases. Murphy's Law says the same thing in a different form—things always tend to go wrong.

The intact cup on the table is a state of high order, but the broken cup on the floor is a disordered state. One can readily go from the cup on the table in the past to the broken cup on the floor in the future, but not the other way round.

The increase of disorder or entropy with time is one example of what is called an arrow of time; it distinguishes the past from the future, giving a direction to time. There are at least three different arrows of time:

1. Thermodynamic arrow of time: the direction of time in which disorder or entropy increases.
2. The psychological arrow of time: the direction in which we feel time passes, the direction in which we remember the past but not the future.
3. The cosmological arrow of time: this is the direction of time in which the universe is expanding rather than contracting.

The thermodynamic arrow and the psychological arrow are interrelated, as the psychological arrow is determined by the thermodynamic arrow. So, they point in the same direction.

If we assume that the universe has no boundary, then there must be well-defined thermodynamic and psychological arrows of time. Together with the weak anthropic principle, all the three arrows will face in the same direction. They may not face in the same direction for the whole history of the universe. However, only if they point in the same direction, the conditions will be conducive for the development of intelligent beings.

Why does disorder increase in the same direction of time, in which the universe is expanding?

The second law of thermodynamics states that the number of disordered states are always much more than the number of ordered states. The example of the jigsaw puzzle explains this appropriately. There is only one arrangement in which the pieces can be arranged to make the complete picture. This is the ordered state. On the other hand, there are very large number of arrangements in which the picture is not complete. These are the disordered states.

To lighten up a bit, let us consider an opposite world in which God decided that as the time passes, the disorder decreased and the universe should finish up in a state of high order. Then such human beings would see the broken cup reassembling and jumping back on the table. That is to say, they will not remember the cup falling from the table and breaking. For them, the psychological arrow would then be pointing backwards and they would remember the events in the future and not in the past.

The psychological arrow of time or our subjective sense of the direction of time in our brain is, therefore, guided by the thermodynamic arrow of time. We must remember things in the order in which entropy increases. That is we measure time in the direction in which disorder increases. Thus, the second law of thermodynamics becomes trivial.

But then the question arises, 'Why should the thermodynamic arrow of time exist at all?' The questions can also be, 'Why was the universe in a state of higher order at the beginning? Why is it not in a state of disorder at all times? Wouldn't that be more probable? Also, why is the direction of time, in which the disorder increases, the same as that in which the universe expands?'

None of these possibilities matches with our observations. In order to understand as to when the curvature of space-time becomes large or in order to understand the beginning of the universe, one has to use the quantum theory of gravity. The theory of relativity is unable to explain it.

It is not the expansion of the universe which causes the disorder to increase but it is the no-boundary condition which causes the disorder to increase.

The universe is bound by a few laws only. The future of the universe can either be expansion or contraction. Contraction will lead to the Big Bang. Expansion will allow it to exist forever.

Some conclusions can be drawn from Hawking's research on relativity and quantum mechanics. There is no role of singularity in it. The universe is complete in itself and has no boundary. If the universe is complete in itself, then there is no place for God.

❑

The Outlook of the Common People Towards Science

Whether we like it or not, our world has changed a lot in the last one hundred years. It is going to change even more in the next hundred years. Some people feel that the changes should be stopped and we should revert to the old and pure world. But history tells us that the past was not so pleasant for most of the people. However, it was not so bad for a few special and affluent people. Even though they were not aware of the latest medicines and their wives had very difficult deliveries. But for most people, it was a life of humiliation, abhorrence, cruelty and filled with crisis.

However, it is a fact that we cannot turn the clock backwards or demolish knowledge and technology. Nobody can stop progress. The advancement in technology will continue on account of the competitive spirits of the scientists, inspite of the paucity of the government funds. Also nobody can stop the scientists from using their intelligence to carry on with their fundamental research. Only dictatorship can stop the future developments. But man's

Delivering Lecture at the Great Hall of People, Beijing, China in 2006

leadership traits and freedom of thought eventually overcome it. At best, it might slow down the momentum of change. Due to science and technology, we cannot stop the changes taking place in the world. Once we accept this fact, then we can make efforts to ensure that the change is for the good.

In a democracy, it is important for people to have at least the basic knowledge of science, so that they can take vital decisions. It is seen that people have contradictory feelings about science. On the one hand, they feel that as science and technology have improved their lives, so their development must continue. At the same time, they distrust it as they are unable to figure it out. Cartoons, which show a mad scientist like Frankenstein working in a laboratory, strengthen their distrust. But most people are fascinated by science, particularly astronomy. Some of the shows on TV like the science of cosmos and other scientific discoveries have been very popular.

To develop curiosity in science, people must have a science background, so that they can decide on the scientific issues. It is essential that they have knowledge of issues like acid rain, nuclear weapons and genetic technology. The foundations must be laid in the schools itself. But in schools, it is taught in a very difficult and uninteresting manner. It is taught in the form of equations. It is true that the learning by equations is a brief and infallible method, but it scares the students. The students mug the answers, just to pass the examination and do not learn about the role which science plays in their lives. Recently, I wrote a very popular book on science. I was told not to include any equation in the book, because, for every equation included in the book, the sales of the book would be halved. I used only one equation in the entire book, that is Einstein's famous equation $E = mc^2$. He later said that had I not included even this one equation in the book, the sales would have been double.

Scientists and engineers present their concepts in the form of equations because they need to be precise. The same concept can be explained by word, shape and picture. An equation is not required.

We learn and understand the basic concepts of science in school. But the developments in science are so revolutionary that by the time the school and college syllabus is framed, it is already obsolete. I never learnt linear biology in school, but on account of developments in DNA engineering and computer science, the society is going to change in our lifetime itself. In the future, it will appear to be influenced by superiority. Popular books, magazines and scientific articles will help us to understand the developments in science. But even very successful and popular books are read by very few persons in the society. Only the television has a far greater reach and has the largest viewership. So, it has the responsibility of teaching science to the general public. Entertainment should not be its sole objective.

What are some of the issues which may arise in the future and need to be addressed by the general public? Today's most vital issue is nuclear weapons. Other issues of the world, that is, food supply or greenhouse effect are not that serious. The cold war sword is still hanging. A nuclear war can annihilate the entire human race in a few days. There are enough atomic weapons amassed to eliminate the world's entire population several times over. A minor error of a computer or a weapon's malfunctioning can lead to a world war.

Even smaller countries possess atom bombs and that is also a concern. So, it is important that the general public understands this crisis and builds pressure on its governments to restrict the stock piling of nuclear weapons. It may not be possible to move all the nuclear weapons to a secure place, but it is possible to reduce their numbers.

It may be possible to avoid nuclear war and avert the other dangers. I trust the simplicity of the general public and am sure that no such eventuality will arise.

❑

Darwin Lecture

In this Lecture, I will inform about what do scientists think would be the future of the universe. Predicting the future is not an easy task. Even I had thought of writing a book to be called *Yesterday Tomorrow—A History of the Future*. It would have covered the predictions made by the scientists. Most of these predictions have been wide off the mark. Still most of us believe that we can study and predict the future of the universe. But I don't suppose it would have sold as much as my history of the past.

In the olden days, it was mostly women who were declared to be possessed by supernatural spirits, who would predict the future. It is more likely that they were put into a trance by some drug. They would start raving loudly and the priests, prophets or the oracles would interpret it as they wished. Mostly, the questions were related to destruction and doom, like when the enemy will be defeated or when a kingdom would fall or even when the universe will come to an end. Definite dates were proclaimed. After the dates passed without the occurring of the presumed incident, explanations would be offered for their failure.

It is not as if the predictions of the scientists are any more reliable than those of the oracles or priests, like in the case of the weather forecasts. But in the case of the future of the universe, we think, on a very large scale, that we can make reliable predictions.

Over the last 300 years, we have discovered the scientific laws that govern the matter in all the normal situations. We still don't know the exact laws that govern the matter in very extreme conditions. These laws will help to understand how the universe began. But they will not affect the future evolution of the universe, unless it recollapses to a high density state.

The relevant laws known to us, that govern the universe, may not help us to predict its distant future. This is because the solutions to the equations of physics may exhibit a property known as chaos. A slight change in the starting conditions may make the equations unstable. Thus, even a small change can lead to a completely different behaviour of the system in the future.

Take the case of the Earth's atmosphere, its time scale is of the order of five days, the time air takes to go around the circle of the Earth. So, we can make a reasonably accurate forecast of the weather of the Earth for the next five days. A forecast beyond that will require an accurate knowledge of the present state of the atmosphere and very complicated, almost impossible calculations. There is no way that we can predict the weather six months ahead, beyond giving the seasonal average.

So is the case with the prediction of human behaviour. We know the basic laws that govern chemistry and biology. So, in principle, we should be able to determine how the brain works with the help of the equations. But here also a small change in the initial state will lead to chaotic results. Thus, in practice, we cannot predict human behaviour, even though we know the equations that govern it.

Science cannot predict the future of the society, or decide whether it has any future. The danger is that our power to damage or destroy the environment, or each other, is increasing much more rapidly than our wisdom in using this power.

Whatever happens on Earth, the rest of the universe will carry on regardless. It seems that the motion of the planets around the Sun is ultimately chaotic, though on a larger time scale. This means that the errors in any prediction get bigger as time goes on.

After a certain time, it becomes impossible to predict the motion in detail. We can be fairly sure that Earth will not have a close encounter with Venus for quite a long time. But we cannot be certain that small variations in the orbits would not add up to cause such an encounter, after a billion years.

The motion of the Sun and other stars around the galaxy, and the motion of the galaxy in the local group of galaxies are also chaotic.

In contrast, the motion of the universe on a very large scale seems to be uniform and not chaotic. We observe that other galaxies are moving away from us and the farther they are from us, the faster they are moving away. This means that the universe is expanding in our neighbourhood, the distances between different galaxies are increasing with time.

However, since the time of Copernicus, we have been demoted to a minor planet, going around a very average star, in the outer edge of a typical galaxy, that is only one of a hundred billions we can see. We are now so modest that we couldn't claim any special position in the universe.

We must, therefore, assume that the background is also the same in any direction about any other galaxy. This is possible only if the average density of the universe and the rate of expansion are the same everywhere. Any variation in the average density or the rate of expansion over a large region would cause the microwave background to be different in different directions.

This means that, on a very large scale, the behaviour of the universe is simple and is not chaotic. It can, therefore, be predicted far into the future. Because the expansion of the universe is so uniform, we can describe the distance between two galaxies in terms of a single number. This is increasing at the present time, but we could expect the gravitational attraction between the galaxies to slow down the rate of the expansion.

If the density of the universe is greater than a certain critical value, gravitational attraction will eventually stop the expansion and make the universe start to contract again. The universe would collapse to a Big Crunch. This would be rather like the Big Bang that created the universe. The Big Crunch would be what is called a singularity, a state of infinite density at which the laws of physics would breakdown.

This means that even if there were events after the Big Crunch, what happened to them could not be predicted. But without a causal connection between the events, there is no meaningful way in which one can say that one event happened after another. One might as well say that our universe came to an end at the Big Crunch, and that events that occurred later, were part of another, separate universe. It's a bit like a reincarnation.

If the average density of the universe is less than a critical value, it will not recollapse but will continue to expand forever. After a certain time, the density will become so low that gravitational attraction will not have any significant effect on slowing down the expansion. The galaxies will continue to move apart at a constant speed.

I can confidently predict that the universe will not stop expanding for at least 10 billion years. We can try to estimate the average density of the universe from observations. If we count the stars that we can see and add up their masses, we get less than 1 per cent of the critical density. Even if we add in the masses of the clouds of gas that we observe in the universe, it still brings the total up to only about 1 per cent of the critical value.

However, we know that the universe must also contain what is called dark matter, which we cannot observe directly. One piece of evidence for the existence of this dark matter comes from the spiral galaxies. These are enormous pancake-shaped collections of stars and gases. We observe that they are rotating about their centres. But the rate of rotation is so high that they would fly apart if they contained only the stars and gas that we observe. Therefore, there must be some unseen form of matter, whose gravitational attraction is great enough to hold the galaxies together as they rotate.

Another piece of evidence for the existence of dark matter comes from the clusters of galaxies. We observe that galaxies are not uniformly distributed throughout the space, but are gathered together in clusters that range from a few galaxies to millions. Presumably, these clusters are formed because the galaxies attract each other into groups. We can, however, measure the speeds at which individual galaxies are moving in these clusters. We find they are so high that the clusters would fly apart unless they were held together by the gravitational attraction. The mass required to hold them together is considerably greater than the masses of all the galaxies. This is the case even if we take the galaxies to have the masses required to hold themselves together as they rotate. It follows, therefore, that there must be extra dark matter present in the clusters of galaxies, besides the galaxies that we see.

We can make a fairly reliable estimate of the amount of the dark matter in galaxies and clusters for which we have definite evidence. But this estimate is still only about 10 per cent of the critical density needed to cause the universe to collapse again. Thus, if one went just by the observational evidence, one would predict that the universe would continue to expand forever. But our solar system won't last forever. After another 5 billion years or so, the Sun will exhaust its nuclear fuel. It will swell up as a red giant star until it has swallowed up Earth and the other closeby planets. It will then settle down to be a white dwarf, a few thousand miles across. So, I am predicting the end of the world, but not just yet.

After 10 billion years or so, most of the stars in the universe will have burnt out. Stars with masses like that of the Sun will become white dwarfs, or neutron stars, which are even smaller and denser. More massive stars can become black holes, which are still smaller, and which have such a strong gravitational field that no light can escape.

One might expect, therefore, that most of the matter in galaxies and clusters would eventually end up in black holes. However, some time ago, I discovered that black holes weren't as black as they had been painted.

To sum up, in the normal course, it can be predicted how the universe will behave for some time. But we cannot predict anything definitely. It is very near to its critical density and anything can happen. In short, our predictions are almost like the predictions of the priests or oracles in the past.

❑

Hawking and Hollywood

In one of Cambridge's high and respected localities, twelve teenaged boys and girls had assembled. A man was seated on a wheelchair in front of them. Everyone was in a joyous mood. Professor Hawking was enjoying it quietly. As compared to others, he seemed weak and fatigued—so he did not seem to be a part of the group. He could, however, move his head and his blue eyes shone through his glasses. A nurse was attending to him. She was feeding him and in between wiping his face with a napkin.

As the group started having their food, the waiter escorted a respected guest there. As compared to her age, she looked stunning. She proceeded directly towards the person sitting on the wheelchair and said, "Professor Hawking! I am very pleased to meet you. I am Shirley MacLaine." Professor Hawking was delighted but all he could say was "Hello."

During the dinner, Hollywood's famous actress, Shirley MacLaine, who was seated next to the Professor, kept on asking him questions. She herself had interest in philosophy and

Popular Hollywood Actress, Shirley MacLaine, Great Fan of Prof. Hawking

spirituality. She would regularly keep discussing these subjects with other learned persons of these subjects. She had deep curiosity, belief and feeling for these subjects. She had her own concepts on the human existence and had lots of curiosities in this context. She had studied in depth about the creation of the universe and the existence of God.

She asked the Professor, "Do you believe that the creator of the universe is God?"

The Professor smilingly replied through the speech synthesizer, "No."

After dinner, the young group leaves and they sit in the study room. Then they discuss about spirituality and scientific topics for the next two hours.

At that time, Shirley was more popular than Hawking. She had been nominated for the Oscar several times and she was

Always Popular Prof. Hawking

given the Oscar Award for being the best actress in the film *Terms of Endearment*.

It was evident from that meeting that in Hollywood there was great curiosity and respect for Stephen Hawking's work. A former director of news channel NBC realised that Stephen's book *A Brief History of Time* was a storehouse of knowledge and learning. Garden Friedman had no interest in making a film on Hawking, but on the subject of time and space discussed in the book. For such a grand project, he got in touch with Steven Spielberg's company. His desire was to present the scientific conceptions in the book to the general public through a film and create awareness on scientific topics. He had respect for Hawking. He thought that Hawking could be compared to Einstein. They met in a studio in Los Angeles in 1990. The meeting lasted one-and-a-half hours. The people in the studio had great curiosity about Hawking and, for the first time, their thoughts were directed towards Hawking instead of Spielberg.

The leading research scientists of Cambridge University, were not in favour of the film being made. But still the film was made. For making the film on the life of Hawking, people who came in contact with Hawking, his office and his daily schedule were filmed.

When the last scenes were being filmed in 1990, the news of Stephen and Jane's separation got public. Hawking's smile vanished.

❑

RESEARCH SECTION

Grand Unified Theory

Imagine that you have never seen the universe. Are there any definite laws which describe the universe? Will we able to understand/study these laws during our limited lifetime? According to some physicists, there is a book of laws, which contains innumerable simplest elements.

This book contains the process which possibly explains as to what happened to the universe in the past, what is happening at present and what will happen in the future? According to Stephen Hawking: "The 'Grand Unified Theory' is within my reach and soon I will be able to complete it."

The scientists' efforts to unravel the mysteries of the creation and possible end of the universe are on. What is the formula, which can explain the innumerable activities which are taking place every moment in the universe? Can I understand this formula? Can I work out this formula? Hawking started working on finding solutions to these questions. In the past century, the scientists thought they were close to finding the answers to these issues. Even after the advent of atomic energy, this optimism had been regenerated.

With Queen Elizabeth at Birmingham Palace during a Music Concert

Initially, only protons and electrons were discovered; thereafter, neutron was discovered. Einstein's theory of relativity, the uncertainty principle, certainty principle, etc. were already known to the scientists. Due to this, the implementation of the 'Grand Unified Theory' became even more difficult.

Size of the Universe

Scientists are always eager to seek answers to such questions. There is curiosity in the general public also. Even poets have expressed their curiosity in their poems. "What is the size of the universe? It is the size of one's imagination." Everyone's head size is more or less the same, but the intelligence level is different. So, their capacity to visualise the measurement of their surroundings and the universe will be different. The state of their minds and their development decides the size of the universe. Does man have the intellectual capacity to understand the size of the universe? Is this what they wished to imply?

Then there is the question—which universe are we referring to? Is it the one that we see with our naked eyes, which is made up of our atmosphere and the infinite number of stars that we see in the night? Or is it the grand universe with unlimited galaxies?

Apparently, the nature is not that disordered as it seems. If we try to understand the entire nature in a straightforward and simple manner, what will be the result? The Nobel Prize winner American Scientist, Richard Feynman tried to find it out. At one point of time, Feynman had suggested that they identify some events first by speed, second by energy it possesses and the third by its momentum. But after Newton presented the law on the speed of sound, it became evident that the events which apparently seem different are the different manifestations of the same event. What is sound dissipation? — The vibration of the atoms in the atmosphere and conversion to energy. So, the basic form of energy and sound is the same—vibration of atoms. According to Newton's theory, energy could not be destroyed, only its form could be changed. What it meant was that, in physical state, all these forms are easily attainable because their fundamental source is the same. This is an example which shows that the states which apparently seem different are the same.

Four Forces of the Universe

Think about the universe. What is it? Universe covers humans, vegetation, living beings, air, snow, stars, atmosphere, microscopic bacteria—they are made up of microscopic particles. Atoms consist of protons and neutron nucleus with the electrons revolving around it. There is enough empty space between them. All the particles follow certain laws. Their behaviour resembles the human behaviour. We have four ways to communicate—telephone, fax, e-mail and mobile. It is not necessary that everyone uses all the four options to communicate. All known matter particles also have four means of communication called

'Why Should We Go to Space'—A Lecture Delivered by Prof. Hawking and Assisted by His Daughter Lucy

forces. They are—gravitational force, electromagnetic force, strong force and weak force. Electromagnetic force controls electrons and the nucleus of the atom. The strong force keeps the nucleus of the atom stable. But the weak force produces radioactivity. In the 20th century, physicists have tried to find the definite form and function of the four forces. They have also studied how these four forces are interconnected.

Let us consider the example of the human's modes of communication, once again. The telephone and fax both communicate, but their methods are different. One allows oral communication whereas the other transmits text. This is called unity. If we can combine all the four forces, then a greater force can be created. The theory which tells us the functions of this greater force is called the Grand Unified Theory. This was the direction of Hawking's research. He wanted to find out the basis and form of the universe. His effort was to prove that the universe was in an orderly state.

Grand Unified Theory

It must be understood that it is not necessary that we can explain the creation of the universe in its entirety with the help of the Grand Unification Theory. There are lots of differences on account of the stretched imagination of the scientists—a leap into space. According to Hawking, such an imaginative theory should not contradict known events. If it does so, then it is essential to produce the reasons for it.

To illustrate this, we can give the example of the Superstring Theory. This theory assumes the existence of ten dimensions against the four known dimensions. This is totally contrary and irrelevant to our observations.

It was believed that light travels in a straight line, but Einstein had predicted that light waves will curve when they pass close to the Sun, on account of its gravitational field. Einstein's theory was proved by experiments.

At present, it is difficult to prove Hawking's theories through experiments, with the available technology. Hawking unquestionably believes that his theories are correct, but he needs to clarify the following things, relating to his theories concerning the universe. The grand unified theory faces the following challenges:

1. He must give the example of force and particle unification.
2. What is the status of the boundary of the universe?
3. He must clearly specify how many particles are there.
4. There should be no conjectures.
5. He must explain the universe as it exists.
6. It should be simple and direct, but should be able to explain extreme disorders.
7. It should be able to explain the unification of Einstein's relativity theory and quantum theory.

Prof. Hawkings Unveiling a Unique Clock "The Corpus Clock" at Cambridge University

Einstein's general relativity theory applies to massive stars, planets and galaxies. The theories put forward by him should be able to clarify how gravitation affects these massive bodies? In this context, the quantum theory's application is exceedingly disappointing, and is appropriate only for microscopic particles. Even though according to quantum theory, it is not possible to find out the position and time of microscopic particles like electrons at the same time. But inspite of it, the quantum theory, is important. Both these theories are path-breaking achievements of 20th century.

There is need to unify both the theories, that is to have a grand unified theory, through which we can explain the behaviour of both the massive bodies and the microscopic particles. This will lead us to understand the basics of the universe.

Not all the physicists think that it is possible to develop the Grand Unified Theory. They question the feasibility of developing a theory which allows continuous developments in science. A small box in a big box, and so on, we may be able to reach the smallest box, but we can never reach the last box. Some scientists believe that some events occur naturally. While others believe that God and humans—both are independent in the stake of the creation. Will this independence allow the Grand Unified Theory? Will it grant its acceptance?

In the world of music, there is a change in the notes of the orchestra, yet creative musicians retain their uniqueness. Even in Indian classical music, there are innumerable restrictions of the ragas, but every singer presents his creation using his imagination.

Accordingly, in spite of all the restrictions of the independent theories, all the scientists desire that a unified theory be developed. Hawking's will to develop the theory is not at all weak and he cannot be discouraged easily. According to him, this is man's most important journey—to see how the universe works and how it was created.

It is a matter of great pride that a handful of people are making efforts to understand the universe. People living on an insignificant planet called Earth, in a very small galaxy, are trying to unravel the mysteries of the universe.

In the words of a poet—"A man's miniscule brain will predict the size of the colossal universe."

❑

Expansion of the Universe

We live in a disc-shaped galaxy revolving in an elliptical orbit. Like our galaxy, there are innumerable galaxies separated by vast space—no scientist was prepared to believe this in the early twentieth century.

In 1920, an American Astronomer, Edwin Powell Hubble, after practical observations, discovered that there are other galaxies also, like our galaxy, in the universe. According to him, these galaxies were located very far from us and were moving apart—or in simple language, the universe was expanding. His discovery and research is considered to be the most revolutionary finding of this century.

Further, according to him, the farther away the galaxies are, the greater would be their relative speed of separation. In other words, if the galaxies are at twice the distance, the rate of their expansion will also be double (Hubble's Law). Galaxies, which are very distant from us, are moving away at the speeds greater than the speed of light. Does it mean that every star of the universe is moving away from us? The answer is: 'No'. Our neighbouring planets move in an elliptical orbit; sometimes they

Handicapped Students Meet their Mentor, Stephen Hawking after a Lecture

are closer to us and sometimes farther away from us. In the group of galaxies, it is the space between them which is expanding.

To understand this by an illustration, consider a balloon. Mark dots (assume that each dot is a galaxy) at different places, on the balloon and inflate it. You will notice that the dots are moving away from each other. The galaxies also move away from each other like the dots on the balloon.

In case these galaxies move apart through time (time travel), then in the future, they can come closer also. But it is not necessary that all the galaxies will meet at one point—for if they do so, then the density at that point will become infinite.

This is one aspect of the expansion of the universe. But it is not as if this is the only possibility, it is possible that, in the past, the universe might have been as it appears today or it might have contracted, due to which all the galaxies might have come closer. However, apart from this movement of the galaxies and stars, there is another movement at lower speeds. There are planets which move around stars. It is also possible that these planets were continuously revolving and, instead of meeting at a point, they scattered just before they collided. They scattered and the universe expanded and formed as it appears today.

The question is which of these events took place and why? Was there a beginning of the universe or not? Hawking initiated his research for his PhD from these questions. He got his lead from the concept presented in 1965 by Roger Penrose, Professor of Applied Mathematics at Birkbeck, University of London. In his presentation, he proved that singularities could be formed from the gravitational collapse of immense dying stars. They both did solid work together to prove the "Penrose-Hawking Singularity Theorems." Thus, the term "Black Holes" was coined.

Roger Penrose is an internationally renowned mathematician. He is known for his scientific work in mathematical physics, in particular for his contributions to general relativity and cosmology. He and Hawking shared the 1988 Wolf Prize for Physics, for their contribution to our understanding of the universe.

❑

Gravity and Light

To understand the behaviour of gravity and light, the general theory of relativity has been unified.

Out of the four forces, gravity is the most well-known force. If we throw a stone up towards the sky, it falls down. If we let go of anything held in our hand, it will fall down. If we slip from a swing, we will fall down. All this happens due to the gravitational force. It is natural that if we were to ask whether this force is a strong force or a weak force, the obvious answer would be that it is a strong and powerful force. But this answer is absolutely wrong. As a matter of fact, it is the weakest force amongst all the four forces. The effect of gravitation is generated on account of the massive weight of the Earth, which is made up of infinite number of particles. It is a result of unification. It is obvious that the contribution of each particle is almost nothing. So, to measure gravity, we need very sensitive instruments. The main thing is that this force only attracts and does not repel at all. So, it only grows.

Sir Isaac Newton was the Lucasian Professor (Professor of Mathematics) in Cambridge. In 1979, Hawking occupied this

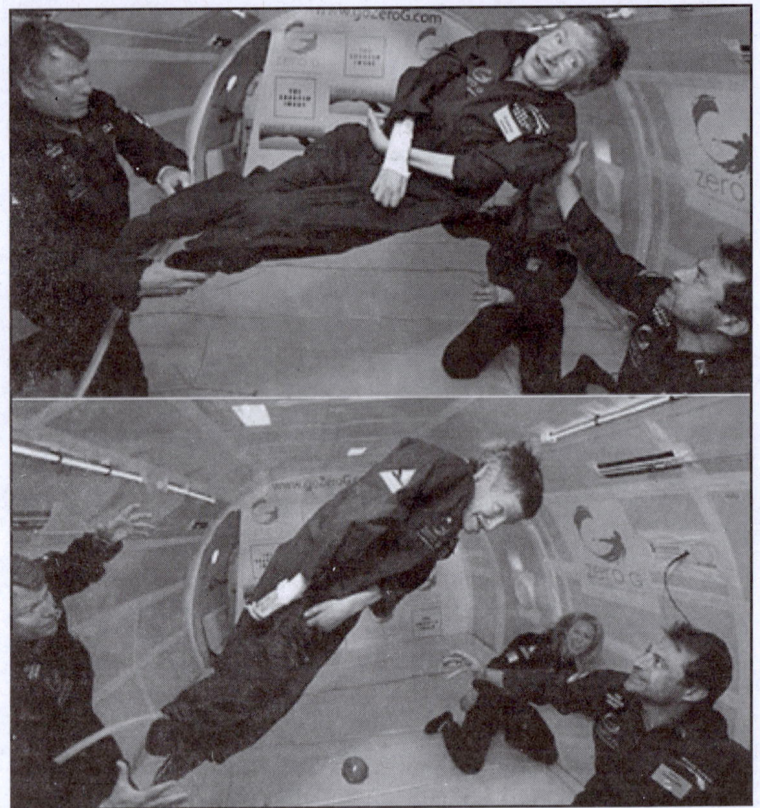

Prof. Stephen Hawking Became the First Person with Disability to Experience Weightlessness in a Zero-Gravity Inducing Flight at Florida in 2007

position. Newton had tried to explain how this force works in normal situations. Imagine that the Moon is isolated in space. If it would not have been stable, if it had been displaced, then it would have moved in a straight line without changing its speed. But Moon is not isolated. It is affected by the force of gravity, so it keeps changing its speed and direction. Where does this force originate from? What is its source? This force is generated by its closest neighbour and more massive Earth. The Moon also exerts a much smaller gravitational force on Earth. That is why, particularly on full Moon nights, the tidal waves are formed in the sea.

According to Newton, the larger the matter or the mass of a body, the greater will be its gravitational force. If the Earth's mass would have been double, then it would have exerted double the gravitational force on Moon. Newton also discovered that the gravitational force also depends on the distance between two bodies.

These theories of Newton were very successful and taken for granted for the next two hundred years. But Albert Einstein realised that there were some shortcomings in the theory. According to Newton, the gravitational force between two bodies depended on the distance between them. Einstein raised the question, "If we consider Newton's theory to be correct and we increase the distance between Sun and the Earth, will there be a change in the gravitational force between the two immediately? Is it possible?"

According to Einstein's theory of relativity, wherever we maybe in the universe, the speed of light will remain the same. It is because nothing can travel faster than light. Normally, it takes eight minutes for light to travel from the Sun to the Earth. That is, we always see the Sun as it was eight minutes earlier. If the Sun were to move away from the Earth, then Earth will not know about it and the impact of this change will not happen for eight minutes. So, the Earth will continue to revolve in its place for the next eight minutes, as if the Sun had not moved. What this means is that the impact of the change on account of gravitational force will not happen immediately because gravity cannot travel faster than light (speed of light is 3,00,000 kms per second).

One more question had remained unanswered. Newton had shown that the planet's orbits were elliptical. But Mercury's orbit, on account of its closeness to the Sun, was found to be different (it has the most eccentric orbit). Newton's laws could not explain it. Einstein's theory was able to explain it.

Einstein had shown by his gravitation theory that when the light from far away stars passed close to the Sun, they would curve on account of its gravitational force and change direction. To understand this, it is necessary to know a little about Einstein's space-time theory.

❑

Space-Time Theory

To say that the universe has three dimensions is an understood/ factful/obvious statement. It would be like describing a six equal sided three-dimensional object in two dimensions. So, in order to understand massive bodies, it is essential to include time as the fourth dimension.

When Einstein wrote his general theory of relativity in 1915, he found a new way to describe gravity. It was not a force, as Sir Isaac Newton had supposed, but a consequence of the distortion of space and time, conceived together in his theory as 'space-time'. Any object distorts the fabric of space-time and the bigger it is, the greater is the effect.

Thus, the fundamental difference between Newton's theory and Einstein's theory is: According to Newton, massive bodies produce a force called gravity; whereas according to Einstein, the massive bodies distort space-time.

According to Einstein, as a large ball placed on an elasticised cloth stretches the fabric and causes it to sag, in the same way, planets and stars warp space-time. A marble moving along the

Hawking Receiving the Prestigious NASA's Royal Society's Copley Medal

sagging cloth will be drawn towards the ball, as the Earth is drawn to the Sun, but not fall into it as long as it keeps moving at a speed. This phenomenon is known as the 'geodetic effect'.

Thus, the planets orbiting the Sun are not being pulled by the Sun; they are following the curved space-time deformation caused by the Sun. The reason the planets never fall into the Sun is because of the speed at which they are travelling.

According to the theory, matter and energy distort space-time, curving it around themselves. 'Frame dragging' theoretically occurs when the rotation of a large body 'twists' nearby space and time. It is this second part of Einstein's theory that has not yet been corroborated.

We are not able to observe these effects due to the extraordinary brightness of the Sun. However, it may be possible to see and study them during total solar eclipse, because, at that time, the Sun is fully covered.

Total Solar Eclipse of 1919

Three years after Einstein declared his theory, such an opportunity was there. A total solar eclipse occurred on May 29, 1919. With a maximum duration of totality of six minutes fifty-one seconds, it was one of the longest solar eclipses of the 20th century. It was visible throughout the most of South America and Africa as a partial eclipse. Total eclipse occurred through a narrow path across central Brazil after sunrise, across the Atlantic Ocean and into south central Africa, ending near sunset in eastern Africa.

Two teams of scientists were formed. One team was being led by renowned scientist, Sir Arthur Eddington. His team was to proceed to Principe Port off the west coast of Africa and the other to Brazil. The First World War had just ended. The air services were just limping. The other team consisting of European scientists loaded all its equipment in an airplane, crossed the Atlantic Ocean and reached Brazil. It was 29th May, the day of the total eclipse. The sky was overcast. The scientists were concerned that so much money and effort might be wasted and they may not get this opportunity again. However, after some time, nature relented. The skies cleared and it brought cheer amongst the scientists. The eclipse commenced, gradually the Sun was totally covered. It was a very precious moment. Within a few moments, lots of snaps were taken. Observations were carried out and experiments were conducted.

Thereafter, the findings of the experiments were obtained. England's leading Astronomer, Royal announced the findings in the Royal Societies grand hall—"The light from the distant stars, while passing the bright Sun, curves on account of gravity—this theory is confirmed." The announcement was greeted with loud applause. It also proved that light had mass. The scientists praised the efforts put into conduct the experiments and declared the findings as a great achievement.

It has been said that this experiment not only proved the existence of gravitational force, but also that gravitation was responsible for shaping the universe. The explanation which Newton missed was uncovered by Einstein. Relativity was proved by experiments. There was a new perspective towards space and time. Like the artistic beauty, the beauty of science is also filled with pride and pleasure. Every research has a poetic element—this was proved by Einstein.

The Discovery of Alexander Friedmann

Friedmann was a Russian cosmologist and mathematician, who helped develop models that explained the development of the universe. In particular, his solutions to Einstein's field equations provided early evidence of an expanding universe, and the theoretical basis for both the Big Bang and steady state models of the universe.

Russian Mathematician Alexander Friedmann

By late 1920, he had belatedly become familiar with Albert Einstein's General Theory of Relativity, which was published several years later in war-torn Soviet Russia. In 1922, he discovered the expanding universe solution to Einstein's general relativity field equations. At first, Einstein thought that the solution was erroneous, but he later agreed that they were in fact correct, and they indeed shed new light on the whole subject. The expansion of the universe was finally corroborated several years later by Edwin Hubble's observations in 1929.

Friedmann's papers from 1924 demonstrated all the three Friedmann's models (describing positive, zero and negative curvature of space-time), a full decade before Howard Percy

Robertson and Arthur Geoffrey Walker published their analyses. This dynamic cosmological model of general relativity would come to form the standard for the Big Bang and steady state theories of the universe (Friedmann's work supports both the theories equally), although the steady state theory was later largely abandoned after the detection of the cosmic microwave background radiation in 1965.

He is best known for his pioneering theory that the universe was expanding, governed by a set of equations he developed, now known as the Friedmann equations.

❑

Black Holes

A black hole is a region of space-time from which gravity prevents anything, including light, from escaping. The theory of general relativity predicts that a sufficiently compact mass will deform space-time to form a black hole.

Imagine that we compress the Earth to its half size. Then, will its gravitational force change? The answer would be 'No' as there is no change in its mass. There will be no change in the Moon's motion around the Earth. But if you land on the surface of this new Earth, you will feel four times gravitational pull as compared to the earlier pull.

But this is an event which is unlikely to happen. Planets cannot become black holes, but massive stars can become black holes. Assume that its mass is ten times the mass of Sun. Further, assume that its radius is five times the radius of the Sun. Then its 'escape velocity' will be 1,000 kilometers per second. (It is the velocity required to escape from the gravitational pull of any body. The escape velocity of Earth is 11.2 kilometers per second). It has a life of around 100 million years. The gravitational force of the star and the pressure exerted by its surrounding gases keep changing. The high speed collision of its hydrogen nuclei in its core (its fuel) results into the formation of helium nuclei. This process is called nuclear fusion. It releases huge amounts of energy that traverses from its interior and radiates into outer space. This is why a star shines. After about 100 million years, the hydrogen present in the star nearly exhausts and it starts contracting. Its gravitational force will keep on increasing. If the star radius is 20 km, then escape velocity will become 3,00,000 kilometers per second, which is the speed of light. So, no light will be able to escape from this contracted star, and thus it appears black. Hence the term 'black hole'.

In 1970, Hawking and Penrose clarified that around the black hole, there is a mathematically defined surface called an 'event horizon' that marks the point of 'no return'. Quantum field theory in curved space-time predicts that event horizons emit radiation like a black body with a finite temperature. This temperature is inversely proportional to the mass of the black hole, making it difficult to observe this radiation for black holes of stellar mass.

Chandrasekhar Limit

The 'Chandrasekhar Limit' is the maximum mass of a stable white dwarf star. It was named after Subrahmanyan Chandrasekhar, the Indian-American astrophysicist, who predicted it in 1930, at the age of 19 years. In 1931, he calculated, using special relativity, that a non-rotating body of electron-degenerate matter above a certain limiting mass (at 1.4 solar masses) would collapse.

Black Hole

Prof. Hawking Getting Ready for His Zero-Gravity Flight at NASA

He was subsequently opposed and ignored by the elite British community of scientists like Arthur Stanley Eddington (who argued that some unknown mechanism would stop the collapse) because such a limit could only lead to the natural discovery of black holes, which were considered a scientific impossibility at the time.

They were partly correct: a white dwarf slightly more massive than the Chandrasekhar Limit will collapse into a neutron star, which is itself stable because of the Pauli exclusion principle.

White dwarfs, unlike the main sequence stars, resist gravitational collapse primarily through electron degeneracy pressure, rather than thermal pressure. The Chandrasekhar Limit is the mass above which electron degeneracy pressure in the star's core is insufficient to balance the star's own gravitational self-attraction. Consequently, white dwarfs with masses greater than the limit undergo further gravitational collapse.

Large Hardon Collider to Disclose Famous Black Hole Theory of Stephen Hawking

Chandrasekhar's discovery might well have transformed and accelerated developments in both physics and astrophysics in the 1930s. Instead, Eddington's heavy-handed intervention lent weighty support to the conservative community of astrophysicists, who steadfastly refused even to consider the idea that stars might collapse to nothing.

But in 1939, Robert Oppenheimer and others predicted that neutron stars approximately above three solar masses (the Tolman-Oppenheimer-Volkoff Limit) would collapse into black holes for the reasons presented by Chandrasekhar, and concluded that no law of physics was likely to intervene and at least stop some stars from collapsing to black holes.

Singularity

From 1965 to 1970, Hawking and Penrose did research together. According to general relativity, there should be infinite density and space-time singularity (a point in space-time, at which the space-time curvature becomes infinite) in a black hole. In such a state, no laws of physics would be applicable.

According to Stephen Hawking's research, immediately after the Big Bang creation of the universe, on account of the immense pressure exerted on some fragmented bodies, they turned into miniature black holes (on the universe scale). These black holes are also called the 'primordial black holes'. Hawking also proved that black holes emit radiations by using relativity and mass theory. This reduces the energy in the black holes. This process is called cloud formation. As the mass of the black hole reduces, its temperature rises. In the last moments of it's destruction, there is a massive explosion of gamma rays. This explosion is equivalent to the explosion of several hydrogen bombs simultaneously.

Practical Uses of Black Holes

The scientists are considering if any practical uses can be derived from miniature black holes. Some of these miniature black holes, which are revolving around the Earth, can be observed by special techniques. The gamma rays which are being emitted by it will be converted to microwaves. These can then be harnessed to produce thousands of mega watts of electricity. The mass of such miniature black holes would be in excess of 4 billion tons. Using black holes of lesser mass could result in its destruction and explosion. Such an explosion in space could lead to calamities on Earth. Scientists believe that the extinction of the dinosaur was caused by such an explosion.

Don Page Fay's Belief

A few important questions arise from Hawking's research. He himself raises these questions–If the universe has no boundaries, then is it infinite or endless? Then it means that God had no freedom to decide on the universe. On account of the belief that universe has no boundary, I do not deny the existence of God, but I only say that he did not have any role in the creation of the universe. It is not right to say that the demarcation of the boundary of the universe decides the limits of his scope of work. If God did not have the right to decide, then what right do we have to decide?

Commenting on the book *A Brief History of Time* in the world-famous science journal *'Nature'*, Hawking's student, Don Page has expressed a completely contradictory opinion on this issue. According to him, God is the creator of the entire universe and also supports it; and his role does not end with its creation. The question of whether or not it had a beginning is not relevant *vis-à-vis* its creation. If we believe this, then it follows that God must have been outside this universe and there will be no need to have a beginning. In any case, he could have started time from the moment of our existence in the universe.

This takes us to philosophical realms. Theoretical physicists put forward challenging questions and present unsubstantiated theories. Eminent scientists put forward new theories everyday and then try very hard to disprove them. Hawking's work has been mostly so. He first proposed that the beginning of the universe was on account of singularity. Then he proved that as the universe has no boundary, it cannot be due to singularity at all. He had suggested that black holes can never contract, but a few years later, he said that they could contract. Hawking keeps saying that he is a scientist with an open mind. His revolutionary ideas shock the world. He does not hesitate to overrule his own postulations, if he finds that they were wrong or were incomplete. That is why, he has been able to make significant contributions to science.

❑

SUPPLEMENTARY SECTION

Trip to India

In January 2001, Hawking visited India. On 15th January, he met the then President of India, Mr. K.R. Narayanan. This meeting became a memorable event, as the President himself said, "This meeting has been a memorable experience." Speaking about Hawking, he said, "He is a symbol of motivation for the disabled persons and hope for the mankind."

Everyone was eager to invite and welcome him. For the benefit of the disabled persons, the National Employment Promotion Council's Chairman, Mr. Javed Abidi said, "We wanted to invite him to honour him. But he had a very busy schedule."

Jawaharlal Nehru University's Environmental Awareness, Disabled and Child Rehabilitation Society had prepared to submit to him signatures of 1,000 students, to honour him for his achievements.

The scientific community was tremendously excited by his visit. More than 3,000 invitation cards had been distributed for his 'Albert Einstein Lecture, 2001' on 'Predicting the Future: From Astrology to Black Holes' in the Siri Fort Auditorium in New Delhi on 17th January. The attendance was so large that

With the President of India, K.R. Narayanan during His India Visit

a full-sized audio-visual screen had to be set-up outside the auditorium for the people, who could not be accommodated inside the auditorium, could also see and hear him. His lecture lasted for an hour.

Later, the lectures given by him at the Homi Bhabha Auditorium in Mumbai titled 'The Universe in a Nutshell' and 'Science in the Future' became very popular. He also replied to the questions from the scientists.

He said that by DNA transplantation, mankind's intricacy will be enhanced but it is necessary to match the physical developments with mature thinking. The biggest challenge to this world may be on account of the population explosion. The population of the world is growing by 2 per cent every year. So, in the next 40 years, it will become double. Everyone needs to unite to address this grave problem. We are bent on destroying the very environment, which helps us to survive. Whenever the environment is devastated, man's animal instincts will be aroused and he will form wild groups. These feelings of Hawking express his concern for the mankind and are really significant and must be taken seriously.

❑

Galileo Galilei, the Father of Modern Science

Galileo's name will always remain on the top of the list of the great and honoured scientists. His discoveries were multifaceted. His works on astronomy and physics were extraordinary. With the limited knowledge available at that time, his contribution was revolutionary. He made original contributions to the science of motion, through an innovative combination of experiments and mathematics. He is, therefore, called the father and visionary of modern science.

He was born in 1564 in Pisa, Italy. Pisa is famous for its Leaning Tower. Coincidently, Shakespeare was also born in the same year. At the young age of 26, he was appointed as the Professor of Mathematics in Pisa University.

He examined Aristotle's theories by different experiments. For one of his experiments, he climbed the tall tower of Pisa. He placed two metal balls—one heavy and the other lighter, in his left and right hands respectively. He then dropped them

Scientist Galileo

simultaneously. The heavy ball hit the ground before the lighter ball. He thus disproved Aristotle's theory.

In 1609, a Dutch Scientist named Hans Lippershey invented the telescope. Using the telescope, Galileo made revolutionary discoveries relating to the solar system and its planets and stars. He discovered stars in the galaxy, found that the surface of the Moon was uneven, sunspots, and that the Sun rotated on its own axis. On 7th January, 1610, his most important discovery was that the planet Jupiter had four main planets like Moon. All the discoveries of Galileo relating to planets/stars advanced the knowledge tremendously. All these discoveries were discussed extensively as Galileo not only spoke about his discoveries, but also demonstrated them to other people through the telescope. So, he used to say not to believe anything about the past theories, but to only believe what one sees by his or her own eyes.

Galileo and Copernicus' research found that the Sun was stationary and the Earth revolved around it. This theory astonished and shook up everyone. It was a complete contradiction of Aristotle's theory that Earth was the centre of the universe; the Sun and other planets revolved around it. This finding reduced the importance of Earth. The Pope punished him for being "vehemently suspect of heresy (opinion or belief that is different from what is generally accepted to be true)" and placed him under house arrest for the rest of his life. So, he had to spend his old age alone. But even while he was under house arrest, he wrote one of finest works: '*Two New Sciences*', in which he summarised the work he had done forty years earlier, on two sciences now called kinematics and strength of materials.

He passed away on 8th January, 1642. Sir Isaac Newton was born in the same year. Hawking was born 300 years later. Galileo gained popularity from his experiment of dropping the balls from the Leaning Tower of Pisa. A Hungarian scientist, Baron Loránd Eötvös verified this experiment in 1909. He showed that effect of gravitation on different objects was similar. There are four forces in the universe. In spite of the fact that the gravitational force was the first force to be discovered, it remained mysterious. Even though it ruled the universe and shaped it, it is the weakest force. In this context, the research of Newton after the apple falling episode is extraordinary.

❑

Sir Isaac Newton

Newton was born on 25th December, 1642 (4th January, 1643, according to new style calendar) at Lincolnshire, England. He was born three months after the death of his father. By the time he took admission in Cambridge at the age of 19 years, he had earned the reputation of a very intelligent student. In the history of science, his research is considered as unparalleled. He is known for universal gravitation, Newtonian mechanics, infinitesimal calculus, optics and binomial theorems. At the age of 42, he wrote the most celebrated work in the history of science titled *Philosophiæ Naturalis Principia Mathematica*. It formulated the laws of motion and universal gravitation that dominated the scientists' view of the physical universe for the next 300 years.

It also demonstrated that the motion of objects on the Earth and that of celestial bodies could be described by the same principles. By deriving Kepler's laws of planetary motion from his mathematical description of gravity, Newton removed the last doubts about the validity of the heliocentric model of the cosmos.

Isaac Newton

Newton built the first practical reflecting telescope and developed a theory of colour based on the observation that a prism decomposes white light into the many colours of the visible spectrum. He also formulated an empirical law of cooling and studied the speed of sound. In addition to his work on the calculus, as a mathematician. Newton contributed to the study of power series, generalised the binomial theorem to non-integer exponents, and developed the Newton's method for approximating the roots of a function.

Newton was exceptionally intelligent; such an intelligent person is born on this Earth, maybe in a thousand years. If any idea germinated in his mind, he would pursue for days and would not give up until the solution was found.

The force, which brought the apple down from the tree, by which the Moon revolves around the Earth and the Earth revolves around the Sun is the same—this, all was proved by Newton. The apple is not only attracted by the ground below it, but also by the surrounding mountains, hillocks and sea. So, Newton suggested that there is the need to unify all the forces.

In science, Newton attained the heights as of Mount Everest and yet was very modest. This displays the greatness of his scientific and human talent. He passed away on 20th March, 1726 (31st March, 1727, according to new style calendar).

❑

The Great Physicist, Albert Einstein

Albert Einstein was born on 14th March, 1879 at Ulm, Wurtternberg in Germany. In 1880, his family moved to Munich. There he had his schooling in Catholic Elementary School and Luitpold Gymnasium. In 1894, his family moved to Italy, first to Milan and then, a few months later, to Pavia, in search of business. Einstein continued to study in Luitpold Gymnasium. At the end of December 1894, he travelled to Pavia to join his family. From 1895 to 1896, he attended the Aargau Cantonal School in Aarau, Switzerland, to complete his secondary schooling.

While lodging with the family of Professor Jost Winteler, he fell in love with Winteler's daughter, Marie. Albert's sister Maja later married Winteler's son Paul.

In September 1896, he passed the Swiss Matura (high school exit exam or maturity exam), with mostly good grades and though only seventeen, enrolled in the four-year mathematics and physics teaching diploma program at the ETH Zurich. Marie

Winteler moved to Olsberg, Switzerland for a teaching post. In 1900, he was awarded the diploma and in February 1901, he acquired the Swiss citizenship.

Albert Einstein

For two years, he could not get a teaching post. With some help, he got a job at the patent office in Bern as an assistant examiner. He evaluated the patent applications for electromagnetic devices.

In 1901, his paper "Conclusions from the Capillarity Phenomenon" was published in the prestigious *Annalen der Physik*. On 30th April, 1905, Einstein completed his thesis titled "A New Determination of Molecular Dimensions" with Alfred Kleiner, Professor of Experimental Physics. Subsequently, Einstein was awarded his PhD by the University of Zurich.

In 1905, which has been called Einstein's Miracle Year, he published four ground-breaking papers on the photoelectric effect, Brownian motion, special relativity, and the equivalence of mass and energy ($E = mc^2$).

By 1908, he was recognized as a leading scientist, and he was appointed lecturer at the University of Bern. The following year he quit the patent office and the lectureship to take the position of physics docent at the University of Zurich. He became a full Professor at Karl-Ferdinand University in Prague in 1911.

During 1911, based on his new theory of general relativity he had calculated that light from a star would be bent by the Sun's gravity. That prediction was confirmed by observations made by a British expedition led by Sir Arthur Eddington during the solar eclipse of 29th May, 1919. International media reports of this made Einstein world famous.

In 1914, he returned to Germany after being appointed Director of the Kaiser Wilhelm Institute for Physics (1914-32) and a Professor at the Humboldt University of Berlin, with a special clause in his contract that freed him from most teaching obligations. He became a member of the Prussian Academy of Sciences. In 1916, Einstein was appointed President of the German Physical Society (1916-18).

Einstein visited New York City for the first time in 1921. He was officially welcomed by Mayor Hylan. During his three weeks' visit, he delivered several lectures at Columbia and Princeton Universities. In Washington, he accompanied representative of the National Academy of Science to the White House.

In 1921, Einstein was awarded the Nobel Prize in Physics for his explanation of the photoelectric effect, as relativity was still considered somewhat controversial. He also received the Copley Medal from the Royal Society in 1925, the Max Planck Medal in 1929 and in 1999 was declared as the "Time Person of the Century."

He was known for his works on General Relativity Theory, Special Relativity Theory, Photoelectric Effect, Mass-energy Equivalence ($E = mc^2$ equation), Theory of Brownian Motion, Einstein Field Equations, Bose Einstein Statistics, Bose-Einstein Condensate, Bose-Einstein Correlations, Unified Field Theory and EPR Paradox.

In October 1933, he returned to the United States and took the position of Professor of Theoretical Physics, at the Institute for Advanced Study at Princeton, New Jersey. In 1935, he arrived at the decision to settle permanently in the United States and applied for citizenship. His affiliation with the Institute for Advance Studies lasted until his death on 18th April, 1955.

His greatest regret in life was that he signed the letter to American President Roosevelt, recommending that atom bombs be made (as told to his friend and great Chemist, Linus Pauling in 1954, a year before his death). However, nobody doubts that he was truly a genius.

❑

Stephen Hawking: Life Summary

1942: Born on 8th January, in Oxford, England. His father Frank Hawking was a Research Biologist. His mother, Isobel Hawking was a political worker. He had two sisters–Philippa and Mary and a brother, Edward.

1953-58: Early schooling in North London. Here he developed interest in mathematics. His father wanted him to study medicine.

1959-62: Specialisation in physics from University College, Oxford. Awarded first class Honours Degree in Natural Sciences.

1963: Started research work on cosmology and general theory of relativity in Cambridge University. At the age of 21, he was afflicted by an incurable disease—motor neurone, that is related to Amyotrophic Lateral Sclerosis (ALS). This disease paralyses physical and speech movement. In spite of the doctors' verdict that he had only two years to live, he continued his research with renewed vigour.

1965: Married to Jane Wilde on 14th July. His first research paper, "On the Hoyle-Narlikar Theory of Gravitation" was published in the Proceedings of the Royal Society.

1966: Awarded the Doctorate Degree. Received research fellowship at Gonville and Caius College. Started research on black holes in collaboration with Roger Penrose of Birkbeck, University of London.

1970: Applying the quantum theory and general relativity, predicted that black holes emitted radiation (Hawking Radiation).

1973: Started working in the Cambridge University's Applied Mathematics and Theoretical Physics Department. By research proved that black holes emitted energy and radiation, even emitted showers of high energy.

1974: The revolutionary discovery titled 'Black Hole Explosion' was published in *Nature* journal. He was unable to move or eat by himself due to his disease.

1977: He was appointed as the Professor of Gravitational Physics at Cambridge University.

1979: He was appointed as the Lucasian Professor of Mathematics (in 1663, Sir Isaac Newton held this position) and was appointed as a fellow of the Royal Society of London.

1985: Started talking through the Voice Synthesizer.

1988: His bestselling book *A Brief History of Time* was published. In 1998, it was recorded as the bestselling book ever in the Guinness Book of Records.

1990: Separated from his first wife, Jane Wilde.

1992: In August, Hollywood film based on *A Brief History of Time* was screened.

1993: Book name *Black Holes and Baby Universes* and Other Essays was published.

1995: His second marriage with his nurse, Elaine Mason.

1998: His book *Stephen Hawking's Universe: The Cosmos Explained* was published, which explains the basis of our existence and other nearby objects.

2001: His book *The Universe in a Nutshell* was launched. In this book, the mysteries over the recent discoveries in physics have been uncovered. His visit to India and delivery of a much debated lecture.

2002: Celebrated 60th birthday.

2003: Production of a comic play with comedian Jim Carrey.

2006: Separation from second wife Elaine.

2007: Celebrated 65th birthday.

Awards and Honours

1975: Eddington Medal by the Royal Astronomical Society.

1976: Hughes Medal by the Royal Society of London.

1978: Albert Einstein Award.

1982: Commander of the British Empire (CBE) by British Queen.

1985: Gold Medal from the Royal Astronomical Society.

1986: Appointed Member of the Theoretical Science Academy.

1988: Wolf Prize for Physics.

1989: Princess of Asturias Award and Companion of Honour.

1999: Julius Edgar Lilienfeld Award from the American Physics Society.

2003: Michelson-Morley Award from Case Western Reserve University.

2006: Copley Medal by the Royal Society of London.

2009: 12th August—Decorated with the America's highest civilian award, 'Presidential Medal of Freedom' by President Barak Obama.

2013: Fundamental Physics Prize by the Fundamental Physics Foundation.

❑

References

- Michael White and John Gribbin, *Stephen Hawking: A Life in Science*, Penguin Books, London.
- www.ffffound.com/stephen_hawking
- www.clipmarks.com
- www.hawking.org.uk
- wikipedia.org/wiki/stephen_hawking
- www.telegraph.co.uk
- www.nasa.gov/.../hawking .html
- Kristine Larson, *Stephen Hawking*, Jayco Publishing House, Mumbai.
- http://www.telegraph.co.uk/news/picturegalleries/uknews/51896069/Professor-Stephen-Hawking-in-pictures.html?image
- www.brainyquote.com/
- www.goodreads.com
- www.mentalfloss.com/
- www.lifehack.org/
- www.refinery29.com/

- www.en.wikiquote.org
- www.hollywoodreporter.com/
- www.time.com/
- www.thejournal.ie/
- www.perimeterinstitute.ca/

❑❑❑